Men of Destiny

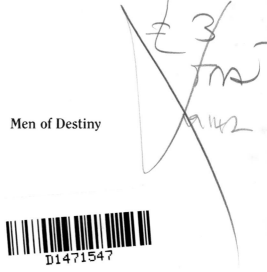

MEN of DESTINY
Peter Masters

THE WAKEMAN TRUST ✳ LONDON

THE WAKEMAN TRUST
5 Templar Street
London SE5 9JB

MEN OF DESTINY

© 1968 Peter Masters
1st edition 1968
2nd edition 1971
3rd edition 1975
Revised edition 1989

This printing 1995

ISBN 1 870855 03 5

Cover design by Andrew Sides

Printed in Great Britain by J. W. Arrowsmith, Bristol.

Contents

Acknowledgements

This collection of great lives was first prepared for a periodical in the 1960s, and has since passed through several book editions. The necessary revision and updating for this new edition has been greatly facilitated by colleagues at the Metropolitan Tabernacle, to whom sincere thanks are due.

Most of the research was carried out at the British Library and the Newspaper Library, Colindale, but the life of Viscount Alexander could not have been written without the kind help of his daughter, Lady Beatrix Evison, who also provided the picture of her father with King George VI.

Particular gratitude is recorded for the help received from the following organisations which located and provided illustrations: The Novosti Press Agency for all pictures relating to Tsar Alexander I; the Wellcome Institute Library, London, for those relating to Sir James Simpson; the Department of Coins and Medals at the British Museum for that of the 'counterfeit' Portuguese banknote; the British Red Cross Archives Division for all those relating to Jean Henri Dunant, and the London Embassy of the German Democratic Republic for most of those relating to Martin Luther.

All other illustrations came either from antiquarian periodicals or from professional sources.

The Tsar's Winter Palace, Leningrad

The Tsar
Who Crushed Napoleon
Tsar Alexander Pavlovich

ALEXANDER PAVLOVICH was by birth and by right *Emperor of all Russia*, dominating his massive land with the undisputed sway of a dictator. It was Alexander's Russia which, despite the most crushing setbacks, set the scene for the liberation of Europe from the iron grip of Napoleon, ushering in his momentous fall. Yet for all his regal power, Tsar Alexander underwent an experience at the age of thirty-six which so humbled and overpowered him that it changed the whole course and character of his life.

Alexander was the son of Emperor Paul — a brutal tsar who produced such chaos in Russia that most people thought him insane. As Grand Duke and heir to the throne, Alexander saw very little of his notorious father. He was completely educated and trained by a Swiss tutor who taught him to scorn Christ as 'a Jew from whom the sect of Christians take their name'. On one of the very few occasions when the future tsar went into his father's presence, kneeling before the throne, the Emperor kicked him savagely in the face. It was a typically irrational outburst of violence. Even countesses had been flogged at his command.

As Paul's cruelty increased, he began to feel afraid for his safety and built a powerful fortress-palace in St Petersburg where he could rest behind walls fifteen-feet thick. But it was almost inevitable that by the time Alexander was twenty-four a palace revolution had been arranged to assassinate his father, and the thickest walls could not protect the tsar from his own palace staff. One night in 1801, sixty palace officials rushed into his bedroom, murdered him, forced his physician to sign a false death certificate, and went out to proclaim Alexander as tsar.

The son commenced his reign with idealistic thoughts of being the great reformer of the land. He dismissed all the old ministers of state and gathered round him a group of young intellectual friends who were officially designated, 'The Committee of Public Safety'. Daily, they held sessions to discuss issues such as the liberation of the serfs and the countless problems involved in bringing a backward nation to freedom and advancement. But they all lacked the dynamic and practical ability to table effective legislation, and after two years their hypothetical discussions became pointless and they miserably faded out.

Young Alexander's own capacity to direct a government fell far short of his dreams, and so, growing rapidly disheartened and disillusioned, he opted out of political involvement and directed his attention to seeking a mistress. Although he was married to Princess Elizabeth of Baden — a marriage arranged by his parents when he was sixteen — he shrugged off the depressing scenes of palace affairs by making daily visits to Princess Marie Naryshkin. In no time he had completely turned his back on his fair-haired, quietly behaved wife, to spend almost all his time with Naryshkin.

Being the tsar, his unfaithfulness in marriage and his lack of religious convictions made no difference to his having absolute control over the Russian Church. So, when a new primate was required, he followed his whim by appointing his boyhood friend Prince Galitsin, a rich young man, notorious for his outrageous public life.

As time went by and Alexander became more accustomed to wielding the power of an emperor his self-confidence grew into outright arrogance and conceit. Frequently resplendent in the uniform of the Royal Commander of the Imperial Army, and very conscious of his striking appearance, he spent a great deal of time impressing the nobility. When he tired of that he decided to widen his audience by going into foreign affairs, a sphere which greatly interested him.

As one who hated the ambitions of Napoleon — Emperor of France and avowed conqueror of Europe — the young tsar tried to persuade Austria and Prussia to help him in withstanding Napoleon. The mindless brutality of the old tsar had certainly been replaced with a subtle cunning in Alexander. He was in his element manipulating foreign powers, even to the extent of wresting five million pounds from Britain to assist in dealing with the French. When it came to practical warfare, however, Alexander was inept. While he dreamed of leading his army to glory, and of being acclaimed the liberator of Europe, he did virtually nothing about the equipment, training and discipline of his troops. When, for example, Napoleon moved his armies against Austria, Alexander wasted time on a round of state visits to various royal families making boastful predictions.

Eventually, in 1806, the moment came when Russian and French forces confronted each other, Russia's troops being commanded by the cynical old General Kutusov, who had already resigned himself to defeat. Alexander arrived on the scene as hostilities began, bringing with him muddle and confusion. It was his first and worst attempt at directing a military campaign. He even managed to become detached from his headquarters staff, very narrowly escaping the final humiliation of capture by the French. In the event he had to flee from the battlefield in the knowledge that his army was being utterly routed.

Alexander returned to St Petersburg covered with shame. There, with his pride bruised and his dreams of glory lying in rags, he began to see the ugly side of his life — his conceit, his immorality, and the selfish emptiness of his ambitions. As he brooded on these things he began to be greatly troubled by what had recently happened to his friend, Prince Galitsin. The prince, soon after Alexander appointed him to the primacy of the Russian Church, had begun to feel conscience smitten about his immoral, playboy way of life, and had started reading the Gospels to see what they were all about. As he read, he realised the seriousness of their message, and came to regard himself as a lost and guilty sinner in the sight of a holy God. Then, after a period of earnest seeking for God, he made a public statement saying that he had undergone an experience of conversion, and that this had made him an entirely new person.

Alexander was jarred by Galitsin's experience. The most abandoned, irreverent man of all his boyhood friends now talked about *knowing* a living Saviour. One day Galitsin challenged the tsar, saying, 'Have

Alexander I

you ever read the Gospels?'

'No,' replied the tsar, 'I've heard fragments in church, but I cannot say that I have really read them. I have always been too busy.'

Now, however, in his time of shame and public derision, Alexander thought much about Galitsin, and in the secrecy of his royal bedroom he started to read the Bible. Soon he was writing to Prince Galitsin,

'This book which you put into my hands has opened up to me a new world.' From that time Galitsin became a regular visitor to the palace, for Alexander had started to search for the meaning of life and eternity. But the search was to take him some time.

Time was something Alexander did not have. He had struck out at the lion Napoleon, and the day of reckoning was coming. Napoleon, following their first encounter, had gone on to devastate the Prussian army and take possession of Berlin. Alexander had no time to lose. He must stop Napoleon soon or in no time his troops would be on Russian soil. Hurriedly the tsar made his second attempt to defeat the lion of Europe. 120,000 Russian troops supported by nearly 500 heavy guns marched into Northern Poland where they struggled against the French for six months. But the Russian effort ended in dismal failure, and Alexander had to agree to talk peace with his enemy.

He met Napoleon in June 1807, on a sumptuous, specially built houseboat. To the amazement of the world the two bitter antagonists seemed to become the closest of friends; so much so that they arranged not merely an armistice, but a solid pact of unity to stand together against all enemies. Alexander, however, was doubtless buying time to rebuild his army and to plan a further offensive.

As the tsar went on down life's pathway personal tragedy brought him back once again to think about the existence of God and the purpose of life. His little daughter — the second and only surviving child born to Princess Elizabeth — developed tuberculosis and died. He had been unfaithful to his wife, but their sorrow brought them together again, and Alexander became more than ever aware that Someone infinitely greater than he held the keys to life and eternity.

Once again, the shadow of Napoleon fell across his reign. The French emperor had decided to conclude his humiliation of Austria and called upon the tsar to fulfil the terms of their pact by providing troops to assist him. Alexander was dismayed, never expecting that he would be held to his pact. There was no alternative but to mobilise an army to help the French, but the cunning tsar took so long about it that the French won their war unaided, entering Vienna in triumph while the Russian troops — moving at a snail's pace — were still crossing Poland.

Once back home, Alexander began building a very much larger army in absolute secrecy. With his chiefs of staff he planned steadily for the day when he would draw the French on to Russian soil, and defeat them at last. But Napoleon anticipated their strategy and commenced his invasion long before the Russian preparations were complete.

It was a day of near panic in the court of St Petersburg when reports began to come in of the mighty columns of men moving northwards to the Russian frontier. As war approached the tsar found himself in a very different frame of mind than in previous engagements. Gone was the arrogant liberator of Europe, fighting for personal glory. In his place was a shrewder man, very subdued, conscious of the grim cost of war, carrying a great weight of responsibility for the lives of his men, and fighting not merely for prestige, but for the defence of his people. As Napoleon drew near, Alexander turned to God in prayer.

In the autumn of 1812, the French army reached Borodino, on the Moscow road. There, in one of the bloodiest battles of all history, General Kutusov vainly sought to hold back the invaders. For hours artillery roared ceaselessly, cavalry units charged, and foot soldiers clashed in hand to hand fighting. 'Never,' wrote a French diplomat, 'did a battle cost the lives of so many generals and officers.' Shattered by artillery, cut down by cavalry and bayoneted by infantry, the Russian lines at last yielded and Kutusov gave the command to retreat. At last, Napoleon breasted the Hill of Sparrows and saw before him in the distance, lit up by brilliant sunshine, the great domes and shining copper spires of Moscow.

Inside the city there was feverish activity as the entire population prepared to leave, taking as much as they could with them. Then they left it to Napoleon — a desolate and forlorn Moscow. There was no surrender by the city; there was no plea for terms; there was just nothing. Indeed, within hours of Napoleon's entry, the city was mostly in flames — the fire being started either by agents of Count Rostoptchin, Russian ex-Governor, or by accident.

In St Petersburg, every noble family thought the war was lost and blamed the tsar for the catastrophe. For Alexander, however, the flames and death of Moscow, pride of Russia, was not only the beginning of victory, but it brought his search for God to a climax. He realised that the abandoning of Moscow could lead to the defeat of Napoleon by causing his army to be detained in Russia until the merciless winter closed in, and this was precisely what happened. On a spiritual level, it suddenly dawned on Alexander that this was also a parable of his own situation before God. Through the loss of Moscow, the pride of Russia, the country could be saved. Similarly, if he were to renounce his own pride and self-love, then *he* could be 'saved' by God — just as Prince Galitsin had been. He realised that he must *die*

Above: Kutusov's war council at Borodino
Below: Alexander enters Paris, 1814

to his old life. His pomp and love of self-gratification must be laid down at the feet of the Lord, so that his prayers for forgiveness and conversion could be heard.

The words spoken by Christ came into his mind, *Except a corn of wheat fall into the ground and die, it abideth alone: but if it die, it bringeth forth much fruit. He that loveth his life shall lose it; and he that hateth his life in this world shall keep it unto life eternal (John 12.25).* He realised in a moment that he could do nothing to earn or deserve the experience of conversion, but he must just fall down before God in sincere repentance, and lay in the dust the old lifestyle and desires that ruled him. He must come to God as a lost and guilty sinner, pleading for a new life, with new spiritual faculties which would bring him into conscious touch with the Lord.

For the first time in his life Alexander prayed prayers that God was ready to hear. For the first time he was truly humble and repentant, finding the truth of David's words, *a broken and a contrite heart, O God, thou wilt not despise (Psalm 51).* God answered his prayers, and from that moment, he was no longer a seeking soul, but a man who knew and walked with his Saviour.

Napoleon waited five weeks in Moscow for surrender. Twice he sent word to Alexander offering peace terms, but he received no response. Then, with his supplies exhausted, he led his army out of Moscow to face near total destruction by the terrible Russian winter. The tsar took up his pen and wrote to his great friend and counsellor Prince Galitsin, 'My faith is now sincere and ardent. It grows firmer every day and I taste joys of a kind I never knew before. For several years now, I have been seeking my way. The reading of the Scripture, which I know very superficially, has done me a benefit which is not possible to express in words. Pray to the Almighty Father, and to our Lord Jesus, and to the Spirit...that They may guide me and confirm me in the only way of salvation.'

Immediately after Napoleon's failure in Russia Alexander secured a treaty with Prussia and continued southwards to pursue him. Napoleon responded by hurriedly recruiting a fresh army, and it took Alexander's skill as a negotiator to bring other nations into the war, and several grim engagements, before Napoleon was driven back on to his native soil.

Alexander called his commanders together to consider whether they should locate and destroy Napoleon's remaining army, or go directly to Paris to seize control. The generals disagreed, and while they debated, the tsar slipped out of the room. He later recorded, 'In my heart I had an irresistible desire to place everything in the hands of God. The Council of War was still going on. I left it for a moment to retire to my room. Then I fell on my knees and poured out my heart to the Lord...'

The tsar returned to his generals to say, 'My decision is taken — we shall march at once on Paris.' Paris surrendered without violence to Alexander in March 1814. The tsar imposed no humiliation or reprisals, for he was now a Christian as well as a military commander. All he desired was the removal of Napoleon to exile on the Isle of Elba, and then France could go free.

The Alexander who returned to direct the affairs of his land had become, like Prince Galitsin, a new man. Dr Tarassar — his second physician — thought that he spent far too long every morning in prayer than was good for his health! He was by now fully and

Gallery of the 1812 war in the Winter Palace
(Hermitage Museum)

completely reconciled to Princess Elizabeth, and together they renounced the gross luxury and excesses of royal life to live in a substantially plainer house with considerably fewer attendants. They also gave great support to the Bible Society of Russia, founded by Prince Galitsin to bring the Scriptures into the hands of the poor.

In the last ten years of his reign Alexander negotiated the so-called 'Holy Alliance', established a university system in Russia with seven large colleges, founded a system of over 2,000 local schools, set up 200 gymnasia for the health of youth, emancipated the serfs of the Baltic provinces, established a national corn storage plan for the relief of peasants in depression, and cut government expenditure sufficiently to abolish the income tax burden on the poorer classes.

These reforms were at the time considered well nigh impossible in the Russian situation, and their achievement was more than sufficient evidence of the tremendous compassion and tenacity of the converted tsar, who ruled over a backward and often barbaric nation with no single minister of state who was worthy of his lofty aims and intentions.

Behind Alexander's back, government officials practised injustice and tyranny, cultivating private corps of secret police and spies to implement their intrigues and to protect their corrupt interests. That was the 'natural' and 'normal' climate in governmental circles in early nineteenth-century Russia. But Tsar Alexander was no longer a product of his environment. He now had the character of a Christian believer stamped upon his heart. Accordingly he became the most kindly, feelingful ruler the Russian people had ever had. He moved freely among his people, and knew particularly well the different congregations of Christians in his main cities, even down to a single family of evangelical Quakers worshipping in St Petersburg.

The Christian tsar died in 1825, having moved from arrogance and failure to repentance and success, proving the words of the Bible, *Humble yourselves therefore under the mighty hand of God, that he may exalt you in due time (1 Peter 5.6).*

Bowers of the Antarctic
Lieut 'Birdie' Bowers

THE NAME OF HENRY BOWERS claimed an indelible place in the annals of exploration and discovery on the day in March 1912, when — with Captain Scott and Dr Bill Wilson — he lay down for the last time in a tiny tent in a swirling blizzard, on the return journey from the South Pole. Bowers was just twenty-eight and, in the opinion of all, had been one of the outstanding men of the expedition. According to Scott he always emerged as the fittest after the most gruelling physical ordeals. Wilson found him the most reliable. Sir George Green admired his amazing memory; and they all depended upon his irrepressible cheerfulness to keep them going through the very worst moments.

Bowers came from a tough, Scottish seafaring family. His father, Captain Alexander Bowers, had sailed race-winning clippers, and had penetrated further up the Yangtze-Kiang than any other Westerner. He had founded ports, and been a representative of the Indian Government in seeking to open up trade with Burma. But the active life of this generous, open-hearted captain was cut short by the rigours of the sea. He left behind two little girls, one boy, and a sorrowing

Lieutenant Bowers, January 1911

widow who eyed her son and hoped he would never follow his father into a career on the sea.

Mrs Bowers brought up her family in a large house in Sidcup, just south of London. Every morning before breakfast they sang a hymn, read a chapter from the Bible, and had prayers together. The children were brought up to know the meaning of the

Cross of Christ and to trust His atoning death as the only way by which sins could be forgiven. Their mother often told them how their father had lived and died a fervent Christian, but she never mentioned the sea, for fear that the seed of desire might be planted in young Henry's heart. One morning, however, Mrs Bowers walked into Henry's bedroom, and saw pinned up over his bed a large picture of a ship in full sail. In that moment her worst fears were realised; she knew that her boy would one day enter the navy. It was a great act of motherly self-sacrifice which took Mrs Bowers to the naval training school *HMS Worcester*, to have Henry admitted as a cadet. He was fourteen, a short stocky boy, with a wild shock of reddish hair and a very prominent, beak-like nose.

The routine of *HMS Worcester* was vastly different from that of a grammar school. Scrubbing, swabbing, and cleaning ship were the basic ingredients, along with strenuous activities designed to harden boys into officer material for large sailing vessels. In the long dormitories below deck, Bowers got a reputation as 'the best tempered boy in the world'. His best friend on the ship remembered him in these words: ' . . . the strongest and best character I have ever known. It was his never-failing practice during the whole time he was aboard the *Worcester* to sit at one of the school desks on the main deck — before the whole ship's company — and read his Bible for a quarter of an hour every evening, during the time that we used to set apart for "slewing round".'

Bowers passed out of the *Worcester* at sixteen, with top grade passes in his theory and seamanship examinations, and started his practical apprenticeship in the merchant navy by joining a four-masted barque, the *Loch Torridon*. In this massive windjammer, just before the turn of the century, the excited young apprentice set out on his first voyage to Australia. Sharing a cabin with another trainee, he found himself constantly on duty. 'Work never stops,' he wrote home. When he was not performing the naval ritual of scrubbing and painting he was assigned to the acting mate to learn navigation.

The apprentices' cabin was nothing more than a hut, built on the main deck, which played host to every wave that ventured on board. When the seas were running high everything the boys had was afloat, but they were still proud of their ship because it could pass almost everything else under sail.

The captain was a terrifying figure, with steel-grey eyes that could wither up the most hardened seamen who came up against him. Bowers himself made outstanding progress, even winning the esteem of his notoriously hard-to-please skipper. He was eighteen and still only an apprentice when the captain made him third mate with authority over the crew. Although it was his third voyage to Australia, things were not easy as the *Loch Torridon* crew hated their captain and were only too ready to vent their feelings on a raw, inexperienced junior officer.

Matters grew even worse when the first mate, after a row with the captain, stalked off to his cabin and remained there for the rest of the voyage. At the same time the second mate went sick, leaving Bowers in the position of first officer under the captain. Storms in the South Atlantic saw him up aloft, high in the swaying rigging, leading the work of making fast huge sails. When dismal ocean mists and relentless driving rain persisted for days on end, it fell to Bowers to hold up the morale of a depressed crew. Nearness to the Antarctic circle found him at the ship's rail

listening to the cries of seabirds — penguins perhaps
— with a strange longing to be with those early polar
explorers who were so much in the news. 'This has
not been an easy voyage,' he wrote home. 'It seems
splendid to be made third mate, and a big step after
only two years an apprentice...but the skipper is out
against his officers and is difficult to get on with.'

With his life filled with the activity and responsibility of an acting first mate, Bowers began to let his
mind feast on ambitions. The world is a wonderful
place, he mused, and the opportunities seem limitless.
Yet at the same time he found himself shuddering at
the seamy side, the rottenness of the world, as he
rubbed shoulders constantly with men who would
have been expelled from anywhere except a prison or
a merchant ship. When the *Loch Torridon* docked at
Adelaide, he wrote, 'The steward has deserted; we are
getting ready for sea again. I went up to the city to
extract the cook from jail, and brought him aboard in
the afternoon. We are getting our new crew dumped
aboard — all drunk.'

His mind raced through ambitions and doubts
together. 'I must get on,' he thought. Was the world
really so much a sinful world as he had grown up to
believe? Would only those people who trusted in a
Saviour and lived to serve Him be saved? Even while
Bowers wrestled with his thoughts, he had to prepare
his ship for the return journey round the Horn — and
home. All hands were called, the anchor hauled up,
the sails set, and the great steel-hulled windjammer
was off again. With the flurry of activity over and the
ship on a steady course, the acting first mate returned
to his spiritual struggle; on the one side: the world; on
the other side: the unseen Lord Jesus Who, Bowers
believed, had so loved him as to die on a bitter cross to

The 'Terra Nova' held up in the ice pack

bear the punishment of his sins. To which would he commit himself?

'I seemed to get into a quagmire of doubts and disbeliefs. Why should we have so many disappointments when life is hard enough without them? Everything seems a hopeless problem. I felt I should never get out, there was no purpose in it. Suddenly, the Lord Himself seemed to step in.

'One night on deck, when things were at their blackest, it seemed to me that Christ came to me and showed me why we are here, and what the purpose of life really is. It is to make a great decision — to choose between the material and the spiritual. While just on the point of choosing the world for good, a possibility which my early training had long kept at bay, Christ revealed Himself to me, not in a vision; not after hearing emotional preaching, but away at sea. Beside Him, the world at its best was nothing, not even life itself. He filled my whole horizon...who could refuse to stick up for such a Friend, Who even knew him afar off?

'It is very difficult to express in words what I suddenly saw so plainly, and it is sometimes difficult to recapture it myself. I know too that my powerful ambitions to get on in this world will conflict with that pure light that I saw for a moment, but I can never forget that I did realise, in a flash, that nothing which happens to our bodies really matters.' Ever afterwards, Bowers looked back upon this intense experience as the time when the Lord met with him, a weak believer, to confirm him in the trust of his childhood, and to lead him on.

He had one more voyage in the *Loch Torridon* before leaving sail for steam, a voyage which broke all records to make the fastest Pacific crossing for sixteen years. Then he joined the *SS Cape Breton* bound for New York. It was not as good a post as he had hoped for, but by now Bowers clearly felt the unseen hand on his life. In advising his sister about her future, he wrote: 'Are you finding, like I did, that taking too much thought for the future only makes disappointment worse? As I have had enough of taking my future into my own hands, I will just leave everything to the One Who knows my ultimate end already.'

Bowers was in New York, aged twenty-one, and still serving on the *SS Cape Breton*, when he received a telegram telling him that he had been gazetted as a sub-lieutenant to the Royal Indian Marine Service. It was a coveted distinction to be transferred from the merchant service to the RIMS and Bowers knew that the Commandant of *HMS Worcester*, his old training ship, must have arranged it.

When he returned to England, he went straight to the *Worcester* to express his gratitude, and while there, was introduced to Sir Clements Markham, the 'father' of Captain Scott's *Discovery* expedition. The Commandant turned to Sir Clements and indicating Bowers said, 'Here is a man who will be leading one of those expeditions some day.' Sir Clements looked long and hard at the young officer. The remark lodged deeply in his mind.

The Indian navy was a far cry from windjammers battling round the Horn, or smoky steamers churning their way across the Atlantic. Bowers found himself posted to a shallow-bottomed gunboat patrolling the Irrawaddy River. Here, ships anchored by tying up to trees, and navigation depended on the vigilant steering of officers who knew every bend and whirlpool in the river. Clouds of mosquitoes hovered everywhere in a climate like a furnace. One advantage of service on the

On the Beardmore Glacier

Irrawaddy was the opportunity it gave Bowers to go ashore, where he cycled up mountains to the Chinese border, watched big game in the jungle, found gold in a mountain stream, learned Hindustani, and set himself to master every sporting activity he could. Not surprisingly, he proved too muscle-bound to play squash effectively.

Just as he had gained early responsibility on the *Loch Torridon*, so he obtained it in the Indian Navy. A chain of unusual events led him to the command of the *RIMS Bhamo*, a 200-feet gunboat which was generally regarded as the most difficult ship in the entire fleet to handle. Bowers took the place of a lieutenant-commander so successfully that he became known as 'the comet'. A fanatic for physical fitness, his work output was quite incredible, but he was inwardly far from self-sufficient. 'I have so often called upon God's help in an extremity when nothing more could be done by me, that these things can never be forgotten. I know that I am often blinded to the things eternal in the rush and strenuousness of life; still, I trust that I shall never let go.'

In off-duty weekends ashore he would always be found at Sunday services. Once, after attending a seamen's service in Calcutta, he wrote home, 'The Sankey hymns were really splendid. What good old memories of Sidcup they bring back to me! I always thank God for those morning hymns we used to have together before breakfast. They are indelibly printed on my memory.'

For nearly a year Mrs Bowers had her son on leave at home, now back in Scotland. Then he was appointed to *HMS Fox*, a British naval cruiser with five-inch guns operating in the Persian Gulf, the hottest climate in the world. Bowers was busy chasing gun-running dhows when suddenly, in 1910, he was summoned to Bombay to see the Director of the Royal Indian Marine Service. Apprehensively he stepped inside his chief's office wondering what he had done wrong. The Director greeted him quietly, and held up two telegrams, 'Lt Bowers' services requisitioned for the Antarctic if he can be spared.'

And: 'If he can be in London by May 15th he will be appointed.'

The Commandant of *HMS Worcester* and Sir Clements Markham had placed his credentials and records of service before Captain Scott who, without even a formal application or an interview, passed over 8,000 applicants and cabled Bombay to secure his services. Bowers gasped in amazement and felt convinced that under such remarkable circumstances, God was overruling the course of his life.

The *Terra Nova*, Captain Scott's expedition ship, left Britain in June 1910, with Bowers in charge of all the stores. Very soon, he was standing out as one of the exceptional men of the team. Bowers wrote, 'The person who has most impressed me among us is Dr Wilson... I am sure he is a real Christian, there is no mistaking it, it comes out in everything... he is a wonderful artist too.' Dr Wilson had also made a private note about Bowers: 'A short, redheaded, thick-set little man with a very large nose, is a perfect model of efficiency, but in addition to this, he has the most unselfish character I have ever met in a man anywhere.'

In no time his nose had earned him the nickname 'Birdie', and the party had mutually decided that there should be a 'Mount Birdie' somewhere in the Antarctic. Frequently, Bowers was called into consultation with Scott, who became so impressed with him, that he decided to take him ashore on the landing party. In January 1911, the landing party disembarked from the *Terra Nova* at Cape Evans, to prepare for the South Pole venture. 'Every day,' said Scott, 'Bowers conceives or carries out some plan to benefit the camp... I have never seen anyone so unaffected by the cold.'

As the expedition progressed, Bowers and Wilson

were the principal morale-boosters. Griffith Taylor recalled that Bowers was always bringing specimens of rock to the geologist with some remark like, 'Here you are: here's a gabroid nodule impaled in basalt with feldspar and olivant rampant.' Ponting, the photographer, said, 'No more cheery, joyful soul ever lived than he, nor any more disdainful of hardship . . . from the hour we disembarked in the South, he was

Scott's privy councillor in all matters relating to the important work of provisioning the various exploring parties.'

The team continually met with shocks, setbacks, injuries; loss of motors, ponies, dogs; and terrible weather conditions. Scott paid even greater tribute to Bowers' 'astonishing physique which enables him to continue to work under conditions which are absolutely paralysing to others . . . his intelligence is of quite a high order and his memory for details most exceptional.'

On 18th January 1912, a party of five reached the South Pole — Scott, Wilson, Bowers, Oates and Evans. 'We have fixed the exact spot of the South Pole,' wrote Bowers, 'and left the British Flag there. I have had the honour to be the observer, in fact I have navigated the party here and done all the observations since Teddy Evans returned. Amundsen's people left a tent with some of their discarded gear close to the Pole. They were here exactly a month ago. I am awfully sorry for Captain Scott who has taken the blow very well indeed.'

On the way back from the Pole troubles slowly closed in around the little party, and following the agonising descent of the Beardmore Glacier in February, Evans collapsed and died. 'We can't go on like this,' wrote Scott a little later. 'I don't know what I should do if Wilson and Bowers were not so determinedly cheerful about things.' In March, Oates, who was in great pain, walked out into the blizzard and was not seen again. By now, death seemed inevitable for all of them, and Scott wrote, 'Had we lived, I should have had a tale to tell . . . the end cannot be far.'

Soon, he took up his pen again to write to Mrs Bowers: 'My dear Mrs Bowers, I am afraid this will reach you after one of the heaviest blows of your life. I write when we are very near the end of our journey and I am finishing it in company with two gallant, noble gentlemen. One of these is your son. He has come to be one of my closest and soundest friends and I appreciate his wonderful upright nature, his ability and energy. As the troubles have thickened, his dauntless spirit ever shone brighter and he has remained cheerful, hopeful and indomitable to the end...To the end, he talked of you and his sisters. One sees what a happy home he must have had...'

Bowers had no fear of death, for he faced it knowing the Friend of his father; the Friend his mother had introduced him to as a boy. He had entrusted his life to Christ as Saviour, and proved the reality of His power throughout his short time on earth. His last words were written, on March 22nd 1912:–

Blizzard Camp,
11″ S of 1 Ton Depot.

'My own dearest mother,

As this may be my last letter to you, I am sorry it is just a short scribble. I have written little since we left the Pole, but it has not been for want of thinking of you and the dear girls. We have had a terrible journey back...God alone knows what will be the outcome of the 22 miles march we have to make, but my trust is still in Him and in the abounding grace of my Lord and Saviour Whom you brought me up to trust in, and Who has been my stay through life. In His keeping I leave you, and am only glad that I am permitted to struggle on to the end...'

Possibly within a few hours, Lieutenant Henry Bowers had passed over the threshold of eternity.

Discoverer of Chloroform
Sir James Simpson

TWENTY-FIVE MILES FROM Edinburgh, on the road to Glasgow, is the town of Bathgate. In 1811 it was a small and casual village, where cows wandered up and down the high street with children playing around them. Only occasionally were they pushed aside to allow a coach and horses to clatter through. The village baker's shop was run by David Simpson and his wife, who had a hard time making ends meet for their daughter and six sons. In fact they had only just steered clear of bankruptcy when their seventh 'great event' came, and the village doctor delivered James Simpson.

James was only nine years old when his mother died, leaving his sister to take up the household reins. The children grew up very poor but very closely-knit as a family. James became a rugged, stocky sort of boy with a taste for anything vigorous, and with a particular flair for books. By thirteen, he was clearly the scholar of the family, and the others decided to make him 'their' student and to support him at college. In 1825, Edinburgh University duly gained another hard-up student, fourteen-year-old Simpson. Two

years of study sped by before he decided to begin a
medical course.

The medical students worked in the Edinburgh
Royal Infirmary where, on the top floor, was situated
one of the most famous operating theatres of the day
— famous because Robert Liston was the surgeon,
and Liston was the man who could amputate a limb
faster than anyone else.

On his first day as a medical student Simpson took
his place with the spectators round the operating
table. There were no clean antiseptic walls, gowns or
masks in those days, and worse, there were no
anaesthetics. A patient was brought into the room,
pale with terror, and laid on the table. The assistants
held her down firmly and a bowl was put in the right
place to catch the blood. Then Liston, his black,
gentleman's suit protected only by a small apron,
took up his knife, and with Simpson taut and horrified, he plunged the knife into his patient. Terrifying
screams rent the air, and buried deep into the mind of
Simpson a longing to see the end of consciousness and
suffering in surgery.

So brief was the medical training in those days that
Simpson qualified as a member of the Royal College
of Surgeons at eighteen. For a time he assisted the
village doctor at Bathgate, then returned to Edinburgh to take his Doctor of Medicine degree and to
stay as an assistant member of the hospital staff. He
earned £50 a year and took every opportunity for
research work. In fact, he spent all his energies on
getting honours, and they soon came his way. Because
of the success of his research work, he was elected the
Senior President of the Royal Medical Society of
Edinburgh when he was only twenty-four. But even
while the laurels were being bestowed, he was begin-

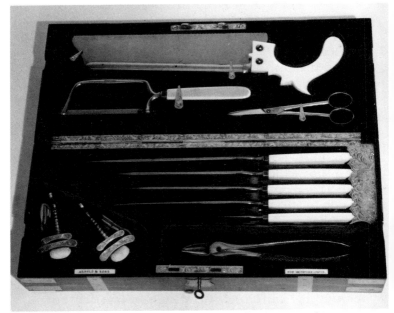

Pre-anaesthetic surgical instruments

ning to feel an undercurrent of dissatisfaction and unrest in his life.

'Yesterday was my twenty-sixth birthday and what a fearful waste of time is summed up in that little numeral...it is awful to think how such a small fraction of time out of these twenty-six years has been employed as it ought to have been. I am always sad on my birthday and yesterday sadder than ever. It was one of those days, those fitful days of gloom, in which the past appeared to me as almost lost, and the future as a labyrinth of vexation and disappointment.'

Simpson was asking himself, 'What is life for?' but his hopes and ambitions were too active for such a fundamental question of life to vex him for long. He believed in this world and he believed that his work would win success and happiness. That was all there was to it.

It was astonishing how much work Simpson compressed into his early life to win success. Aged only twenty-seven, he became a lecturer in obstetrics at the university. In terms of both content and communicational skill these lectures were universally considered brilliant. The word went round and the students crowded into his lecture room to enjoy Simpson's unique illustrations and magnetic personality. With his reputation and wealth growing rapidly, Simpson soon became dissatisfied with life as a lodger and looked around for a house of his own. In Queen Street, he found a tall, elegant house to let and took it, furnishing the downstairs rooms as consulting rooms suitable for his ever-increasing flow of private patients. Even the tradesmen in the city began to take notice as hotel-keepers and others found their businesses benefiting from the numbers of wealthy people who were now visiting Edinburgh to consult Simpson.

Then came an even greater step forward in his career when in 1839, the professor of midwifery at the University died and the post became vacant. Not surprisingly the ambitious young Simpson wanted that post very badly, but he was not the only applicant and a fierce battle lay before him. He set about finding sixty doctors to write him testimonials. Then he had two other obstacles to surmount. He was only twenty-eight, and more serious still, he was a bachelor, which automatically disqualified him.

It so happened that he had been courting a Liverpool girl for some time, and now love and expedience drew together in a letter of proposal. He wrote, 'My dear Jessie, within the last few days I have drawn out a

A hospital ward in Simpson's day

formal application for a professorial chair...I write to make formal application for a wife.' Jessie consented, and to the consternation of his opponents, Simpson ceased to be a bachelor.

The great selection day came and the University Council met together. The representatives from the City Council (all tradesmen) supported Simpson. The academic members were not at all enthusiastic about a mere baker's son, and they supported Simpson's rival — Dr Kennedy. The vote was taken and Simpson won by seventeen votes to sixteen. He wrote home, 'Jessie's honeymoon and mine is to begin tomorrow. I was elected Professor today by a majority of one.'

Simpson's appointment stirred up a great deal of jealousy in the medical fraternity. 'Basking in sunny shallows,' wrote one person, 'was not Simpson's lot. He was seldom out of some big war or skirmish.' As for the students and private patients, they thought more of Simpson than ever, and at thirty-one his earnings spiralled up to £4,000 a year in fees, a vast sum for the times.

Outwardly, Simpson followed the Christian faith, regularly attending St Stephen's Church, Edinburgh, where Dr Muir preached evangelical sermons. But his real opinion of Christianity was — 'good at death but not in life'. One day he returned home from lectures to find his little daughter seriously ill. No amount of treatment seemed to help her, and she rapidly deteriorated. When she died, her father was stunned and jarred into anguish. How pointless and cruel life seemed. Was there a life after death? Once again his mind asked many questions, but once again the buoyant spirits of a man with so much faith in the world carried him back to his work and ambitions. Simpson could not focus his mind for long on the point and meaning of life while there were material things around him to capture his interest.

Then, in 1846, the news came from America that a successful anaesthetic had been discovered — ether. Within months Robert Liston had tried it in Scotland, but the dangers and disadvantages of ether were too great and a more satisfactory anaesthetic had to be found. Simpson joined the struggle to find the answer, and through the summer and autumn of 1846 he and his helpers tried drug after drug, sniffing, tasting and recording the effects on themselves. Eventually they tried chloroform. The local chemist suggested it in the first place but failed to produce a bottle. With typical impatience, Simpson immediately obtained some from another town, but when he examined it he shook his head rather dubiously. 'After seeing such an unvolatile liquid, I despaired of it.'

The bottle lay untouched for a few days until one evening Simpson decided to try it as a long shot. His helpers, Dr Duncan and Dr Keith, set out three tumblers, Simpson poured a little into each one, and then they breathed the fumes deeply. For a moment there was no effect, then Dr Keith began laughing loudly, Duncan danced round the room like a child and Simpson felt very, very drunk. Suddenly, all three lost their senses and collapsed. They had found their better anaesthetic, and in no time it was introduced to the operating theatre to be hailed as a resounding success. Simpson first tried chloroform for a mother in labour. She was so excited about the less painful birth that she named her baby girl Anaesthesia!

The discovery of the anaesthetic properties of chloroform brought Simpson national fame over-night, and yet he found himself unable to enjoy this experience in the way he had expected. Instead, he felt curiously burdened, uneasy and even guilty, as though he had been running away from life rather than succeeding in it. Those nagging questions of his early life; those moments of wanting to know the meaning of it all; such questions kept returning, and he knew they had to be answered.

When certain people attacked anaesthetics on 'religious' grounds Simpson published a reply in which he referred frequently to Bible passages. The result was that he began to be referred to in periodicals as 'the Christian physician', but he knew in his heart that the description was false. He knew that really he worshipped success, and rejected the possibility of a personal relationship with the living God, though he kept his true position covered by a cloak of Christian respectability.

At this moment an event occurred which made a deep impression upon the unsettled soul of this now famous young obstetrician. His closest medical friend, a doctor named John Reid, died after a long illness. Dr Reid had been converted to the Lord Jesus Christ while walking alone in the Cumberland countryside thinking deeply about the Gospel message which he had heard many times through attending churches. He had undoubtedly told Simpson what Christian conversion was and how it must be sought. Simpson had watched as Dr Reid suffered the intense pain of his terminal illness, and had been moved by his extraordinary peace. He had heard him praying aloud to his Saviour, and heard also his dying words, 'The world is behind!' Simpson, whose life depended on this world and the things in it, could not forget what he had seen and heard. More seriously than ever before he began to search for the answers to his spiritual questions. 'I seldom saw him,' said another friend, Dr Dun, 'without being asked the meaning of some passage of Scripture.'

Dr Reid had known Christ in a personal way and Simpson began searching for that same relationship. He began by trying to find a foothold in God's kingdom by his own efforts, and his churchgoing friends were quite startled when he offered to help them in things they were doing for their church. But the time was drawing near when he would understand that the only way to find Christ was to come as a lost and guilty sinner to receive freely the pardoning, life-changing love of the Lord.

Doctors Simpson, Keith and Duncan test chloroform

That understanding dawned when Dr Simpson was called to the bedside of an invalid woman who was a firm Christian believer. As he prescribed a course of treatment, she spoke to him about his soul, and afterwards he was moved to write to her asking for daily prayer. In her reply, his patient challenged him about the spiritual poverty of his rich life, so full of earthly achievement. She wrote, putting these words into his mouth:

'When benevolence shall have run its course, when there shall be no sick to heal, no disease to cure, when all I have been engaged about comes to a dead stop — WHAT is to fill this heart and thought and powers of mine?'

Simpson had asked that question for years, but never seriously looked for the answer. Now, however, he had become acutely aware of the sinfulness of a life which had been one long snub to Almighty God. A battle raged within him. He was addicted to wealth and honours, but he longed for forgiveness and knowledge of God. At last, his struggles came to a head and he found his way to the house of his invalid friend, saying, 'I felt I must go somewhere tonight ... I wish to come to Christ, but I can't see Him.'

The famous doctor was urged to repent of his sins before God and to trust only in Christ's death for salvation. No one who earnestly seeks Christ in repentance is ever turned away, and by Christmas 1858, James Simpson knew that he was a changed man — a newly-converted Christian. His whole attitude to life changed. He found that he possessed a new understanding of God, and of His Word — the Bible. He could pray feelingfully as never before, and God answered his prayers. He felt a deep certainty within that God had made him His child, and he wanted above all else to serve Him and know Him more.

Simpson's conversion caused a considerable stir at the Royal Infirmary. Some of his friends were astonished. One said, 'What a curious psychological phenomenon this step of Simpson's is! I can't make it out.'

In his lecture room, Simpson told his students about his experience, calling himself the oldest sinner and the youngest believer in the room. What difference had his conversion made to him? He told his students: 'In Christ you will find a Saviour, a companion, a counsellor, a friend, a brother who loves you with a love greater than the human heart can conceive.'

Before his conversion, Simpson had been entirely under the influence of this present world. He loved it

Sir James Young Simpson

and lived for it, and he brought up his children to admire it and succeed in it. For someone who considered himself a 'man of science and broad vision' his outlook had been narrowly limited to material things. But after his conversion his ambitious self-love died. He had been given a new start and was concerned about pleasing God. He became anxious that his children should understand life's purpose and come to know Christ also. He also ceased to involve himself in his chief sport — petty wrangles and disputes in the medical world — and became a much more earnest person, more genuinely interested in the welfare, especially the spiritual welfare, of others.

Towards the end of his life, when in his fifties, Simpson was honoured with a knighthood. He had contributed greatly to the advance of anaesthetics by discovering the suitability of chloroform, and it had been his strong advocacy that won it approval, even to the extent of gaining the confidence of Queen Victoria who bore Prince Leopold under chloroform, attended by James Simpson. In his teaching he had laid the groundwork for the advanced study of gynaecology, so much so that some of his written work continued to be the finest exposition of the subject for the best part of a century. Despite all this, when he was asked at a great public meeting what his greatest discovery had been, he replied without any hesitation, 'That I have a Saviour.'

Sir James Young Simpson died aged 58. On the day of his funeral no work was done in Edinburgh and 2,000 people followed the hearse. His words of witness had become very familiar in Scottish circles:—

'We can do nothing to wash away our guilt before God, but Christ has done all that is required. Believe on the Lord Jesus Christ, and thou shalt be saved.'

The World's Most Notorious Counterfeiter
Alves Reis

ALVES REIS WAS EASILY the richest man in Portugal. He had risen from bankruptcy to multi-millionaire status in the space of only two years — success which came to him by courtesy of a famous firm of London banknote printers who supplied him with a fortune in 'genuine' banknotes as the unwitting victims of the world's most audacious fraud. It was a crime which almost enabled its author to take over the national Bank of Portugal. When it was uncovered by chance in 1925, it rocked the nation, led to the disgrace of leading public figures, and toppled the government.

Reis started out in life obsessed by a degree of materialism and ambition which made fraud as essential to his life as everyday speech. After his first year as an engineering student, he abandoned his course, married, and emigrated to the emerging Portuguese colony of Angola, thus evading military service in the First World War. Balding from early twenties, Reis was short, very broad-shouldered, and endowed with an energetic and resilient constitution. Coming from the Portuguese middle classes — his father co-owned a funeral parlour — he was highly literate. He was also endowed with a quick mind and an imagination that was both fertile and rapacious.

'I was twenty-one years old, of a romantic temperament and given to dreaming great things. My short life had already led me through labyrinths of passion and fantastic visions. The selfish and sensual materialism of the times had taught me to oppose all spiritual theories and to seek material wealth.'

In his pocket, Reis carried a most impressive document. It was a degree in engineering science granted by the imaginary 'Polytechnic School of Engineering' of Oxford University. With this forged British degree (complete with gold seal), Reis made truly remarkable progress in Angola, a developing region many times larger than Portugal. His dynamic approach to colonial problems led to one promotion after another, and at the age of twenty-three he had become the colony's top scientific civil servant as well as the director of the railway system. Before long, however, Reis decided that a life in bondage to a state employer was not for him; it was time he became a millionaire. He therefore resigned his position, and formed a trading company which became so successful that within three years he was able to move his headquarters to a prestigious office suite in Lisbon, where he cultivated the image of a brilliant young financier, complete with chauffeur-driven Nash Sedan car.

In Reis, financial ambitions combined with a genuine love for Angola, a region so ready for exploitation. He wrote of it — 'I had sailed along Angola's extensive coastline; I had undertaken many arduous journeys inland, studying carefully the resources of the country, and I was now lost in wonder as I recalled the immensity of the riches of its soil and subsoil. Every kind of produce both of the temperate and torrid zones can be raised there, as though Nature had wished to display to mankind her might and caprice! In the subsoil, gold, silver, copper, tin, iron and diamond furnish the means to make the Angola of tomorrow one of the most prosperous lands of the whole African continent, whilst, to enhance the tale of its natural riches, there are table-lands where white men find climatic conditions second to none in Europe. How the promises of mother Earth stimulate and madden her children!'

Never short of self-confidence or imagination, Reis dreamed of becoming the Cecil Rhodes of Angola, planning and financing great schemes for development and colonisation. But in the early 1920s, a financial crisis hit the colony which threatened to wreck all his plans, and Reis was forced to find an unorthodox way of raising capital quickly. He devised a way of taking over the entire Royal Trans-African Railway Company of Angola, depending on the slow sea voyage of an uncleared cheque! He bought the necessary majority shares — helped by innocent partners — using a cheque drawn on his New York bank account. This gave him a couple of weeks to gain possession of the company, together with its cash reserves and properties, before his cheque was dishonoured. Once in control he was able to utilise the company's resources both to honour his cheque and to finance his other interests. Despite his cunning, the manoeuvre was doomed to failure and led Arthur Virgilio Alves Reis to a damp, dark Oporto prison facing a formidable list of charges.

A remand cell, however, was by no means the end of Reis, who sold everything — home, jewellery, cars — to secure bail, pay newspapers to print a story that he was the victim of a political plot, and bribe lawyers to manipulate the charges. Then, with a few deft 'adjustments' to his company's affairs, his liberty was assured. To garnish his triumph he made sure that his accusers ended up in worse trouble themselves. He was now penniless, but a new project lay before him, a scheme for enrichment far greater than anything he had conceived before.

The fifty-five days spent on remand in prison had not passed without some effect on the young financier, although not the effect the law intended. Sitting day after day in his cell, Reis thought long and hard about his great plans for exploiting Angola. He saw all the financial potential in the mighty rivers, the cheap native labour and the vast mineral resources. Alves Reis would develop it all. 'How can I do it?' he thought. 'Even if I secure my acquittal, my name and my money are lost.'

As he wrestled with his problem, a plan evolved which was both incredible and impudent. Portuguese currency, like most currencies, had long since left the gold standard, and the Bank of Portugal made no attempt to maintain the value of its banknotes. In the previous five years there had been a sixfold increase in the number of banknotes issued by the Bank, and in that period the rate of exchange had moved from eight escudos to the pound sterling to 105! Whenever the government needed money, without any fuss or devaluation, they simply printed more banknotes. Just one precaution was taken. So that the general public would not realise that their money was losing its value, the new banknotes were issued with great secrecy. This provided the key to the Reis plan. He would assume the position of an appointed agent of the Angola government to arrange a secret issue of banknotes. He would select as his 'partners-in-crime' a group of highly reputable rich men, who would work for a percentage, under the impression that Reis was a genuine agent of the government arranging a secret banknote issue. None of them would know that they were party to a monumental fraud.

No sooner was he out of prison than Reis began putting his plan into operation. After his office staff had gone home he worked late into the evenings forging a secret contract between the Angola government and himself. This contract commissioned Reis to secure a vast sum of money to be invested in Angola by outside financiers. In exchange, he would have the right and the responsibility for arranging a secret banknote issue — and for receiving the proceeds. Such a contract would seem plausible to the men whose help he needed, for it would explain how Reis — a private financier — should be given the job of handling official currency.

The most extraordinary and ingenious fraud of all time was now ready to be launched by one who was entirely self-taught in the criminal skills of forgery and embezzlement. By a highly elaborate procedure of lies and intrigue Reis arranged for the contract to be legally authorised — as all Portuguese contracts were — without the legal parties responsible realising its contents. Once he had then inserted all the necessary forged signatures he was ready to bring in his innocent associates.

Karel Marang was a Dutch diplomat and a financier. Adolf Hennis was an extremely wealthy German businessman. Both were intrigued and excited by the idea of lending money to Angola in return for arranging the printing and distribution of banknotes, and both realised they were bound to make a considerable amount of money. It was Marang who travelled to London to arrange the printing of the notes. On

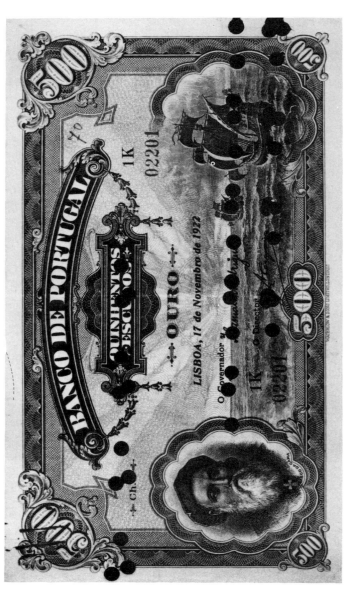

A 500-escudos note of the series reprinted for Reis

December 4th 1924, he stepped into the imposing office of Sir William Waterlow, head of the famous firm of money and postage-stamp printers. Waterlows were the official printers of 500-escudos notes for Portugal.

Sir William, completely deceived by the approach, and by the fake contract carried by Marang, agreed to print 200,000 notes and to maintain the strictest secrecy. The bill for a million pounds-worth of money would be £1,500! The notes would, of course, be printed from the official plates already in the possession of Waterlows, using exactly the same serial numbers which had been used on a previous printing. Sir William Waterlow suspected nothing strange in this as he was told that the notes would be overprinted with the word ANGOLA. A confirmatory order for the work would be communicated to Sir William in the form of a personal letter from the Governor of the Bank of Portugal — or rather from Alves Reis, assuming that illustrious mantle.

In February 1925, Marang collected the first consignment of banknotes, packed in a suitcase and a parcel, and caught the Liverpool Street boat train to Harwich. Being a diplomat as well as a financier his bags carried the orange labels of the diplomatic service, so there was nothing to fear from the customs. Soon the notes were being spread across Portugal by Alves Reis and his agents. They bought vast sums of foreign currency with them, and also opened numerous bank accounts in which to deposit them. In all the major cities of Europe accounts were opened for the laundering of massive deposits of Reis's banknotes.

As time passed and more banknotes were delivered, Reis and his colleagues founded the Bank of Angola

to help distribute the notes, and to arrange investments in the colony. Reis's schemes now began to
take shape. 'I formed a number of companies,' he
wrote, 'and I approached the government with a plan
for colonisation of the centre-land. I also made a
contract with the High Commissioner to build an
important new railway line.' For himself Reis bought
one of the most expensive mansions in Lisbon, the
Menino d'Ouro, or Golden Boy Palace, and gave his
wife a fortune in jewellery.

Thousands upon thousands of green 500-escudos
notes continued to be changed by Reis's agents. Banks
round the world were soon holding vast sums in his
name, and he was acclaimed as the great financial
genius who alone could elevate the colony out of
economic stagnation. Many times bank managers
grew deeply suspicious of the endless bundles of crisp
new banknotes passing through their hands, and
frequently they referred samples to the official experts
at Lisbon. Were they genuine? Of course they were.
They were printed on the Bank of Portugal's own
plates. The mounting fears about the massive amounts
of 500-escudos notes in circulation had to be calmed,
and the Bank of Portugal issued letters of assurance to
all other bankers, later reiterated in newspaper edito-
rials which ran: 'The Administrator of the Banco de
Portugal informs us that there is no foundation for the
rumours current in some localities that there are in
circulation false 500-escudos notes.'

By the time Waterlows had printed notes worth
three million pounds, Reis, as Portugal's richest man,
practically owned Angola, and was buying up the
shares of the Bank of Portugal, having already secured
31,000 of the 45,000 needed for absolute control.
Soon he would own the national bank whose notes he

was forging, and then be above all possible detection.
But Reis had made no allowance for the interference
of the press. A leading daily paper in Lisbon, incensed
by the extravagance and indulgent luxuries of Reis
and his colleagues, began to suspect an enormous
swindle. The paper opened a virulent campaign
against the activities of the Bank of Angola. Then, one
day, Bank of Portugal inspectors swooped on a
branch of Reis's bank to find one great flaw in the
banknotes which had so long deceived them. The
notes were perfect, but the serial numbers were
exactly the same as notes which had been printed
some years previously.

Within hours, the whole fabric of fraud collapsed.
Reis and others were arrested and taken to Lisbon.
Panic seized the country as the news spread that
thousands of useless notes were in circulation. Vast
crowds of people stampeded to Bank of Portugal
branches to change their 500-escudos notes — press
photographs showing scenes of national disorder with
riots and demonstrations in every city square. Anyone holding these banknotes, the most common in
Portugal, found them worthless overnight. From the
family housekeeping to cash life-savings, all was
suddenly worthless.

For Reis, it was to be the fight of his life. 'Determined not to be overcome, I attacked innocent
people. I falsely accused the Bank of Portugal, the
High Commissioner, politicians and financiers. I
attempted to involve them all.'

Almost unanimously, the Portuguese nation
believed the story that their leaders had authorised the
secret issue of banknotes, and were now making Reis
their scapegoat. More than twenty bank chiefs and
government ministers were arrested, including for a

*Alves Reis
out of prison
in 1946*

time, the Governor and Vice-Governor of the Bank of
Portugal, while Reis, from prison, hired the best
lawyers and continued to implicate others in his
crimes. The government in the meantime passed new
laws increasing the prison sentences for fraud.

It took six years to clear away the debris of lies and
false trails spread by Reis before the prosecution had
exposed the truth, acquired impregnable evidence,
and thus arrived at the point where they were ready
for a trial. At last, worn out, penniless, deserted by
everyone, and with only public humiliation and a life
sentence before him, Reis swallowed a phial of deadly
poison which he had kept during his six years remand.
Even that failed, and he regained consciousness to
find himself in the prison hospital.

A few beds away from Reis lay a sick prisoner who
had been stirred to deep thought about his soul by
reading the Bible. Reis recalled later: 'He sought to
prove to me that the Bible is God's book. We had
heated discussions. A conceited desire to prove my

point of view led me to read parts of the Bible. I came across the definite assertion, *Search the Scriptures; for in them you think you have eternal life, and these are they which testify of me*. I then made a systematic, but merely intellectual study of the Bible. I was coldly critical, yet I was surprised to have to arrive at the conclusion that Christ can be traced in the Scriptures from *Genesis* to *Revelation*. He is there as the Saviour, the promise of Whose coming runs right through the Old Testament. My mind became very concerned with the authenticity of the Bible.'

Reis began to worry very much about the existence of God. He wrote to an old friend who was a priest and a scholar in the Roman Catholic Church, and earnestly studied all the advice and literature he received.

Still, the matter of his 'innocence' had to be settled. Fresh forgeries were prepared for him which would prove once and for all that the directors of the Bank of Portugal were his employers. This time the forgeries were accompanied by fervent prayers to God for their success! But instead of success, Reis was seized with a strange compulsion which he could not shake off no matter how hard he fought. It was a compulsion to confess his crimes.

Reis yielded. First, he followed the urging of his friend to join the Church of Rome. Then, after those long years of remand, he stood trial alongside seven associates and his distraught wife. For five hours, Reis made legal history with a speech of confession before the court. All his inborn eloquence manifested itself, creating such an impression that even the Attorney General accidentally addressed him as 'your excellency', and the daily newspapers were provoked to lavish applause. Fervently he sought to demonstrate the innocence of his confederates, but all except one were sentenced. Reis received twenty-five years penal servitude. Up till then he had been on remand — wearing his own clothes and with many liberties within the prison. Now, from 1931, his long sentence would begin with two years in solitary confinement, clad in a convict's uniform, and known by a number.

Back inside the grim walls of the Cadeva Nacional he was tormented night and day by his conscience because of the sentences passed on his innocent dupes. In his anguish he seized the Bible which had lain untouched since his first attempt to study it in the hospital. What could it tell him?

'The Scriptures opened up to me new horizons. The epistle to the *Romans* taught me justification by faith, and *Hebrews* overthrew my views on the priesthood. All I had read by teachers of the Roman Church was so different from what I seemed to find in the Scriptures. Who could assist me in my studies? I prayed unceasingly, seeking light from God. My progress was slow and I was afraid of relapsing to rationalism. I knew of no group of Christians like those depicted in the New Testament. I read in the Bible, *Call upon Me in the day of trouble: I will deliver you.* By His grace, the Lord sent me deliverance.'

Reis had not been praying long for help when he received through the post a bundle of evangelical tracts sent to him on impulse by a British Christian missionary working in Portugal. 'On each of the tracts, which I still treasure, I read, "Anyone seeking information may receive free help by writing to George Howes."' Reis wrote the same day. The missionary visited the notorious criminal and placed at his disposal all his books.

It was while reading an article given him by George Howes that Reis came fully to understand how he should seek God for true conversion. 'I read and re-read that article, and my soul vibrated with profound and irrepressible joy.' The article explained the need for sincere repentance; the impossibility of earning God's pardon; the necessity of trusting in the work of Jesus Christ on Calvary when He took the punishment of sin on behalf of sinners, and the need to cry out to Him for a completely new life.

Reis, from that moment, threw away his pride — in his crimes, his ingenuity, his imagined virtues — and began to ask God to take him and change him. Now he began to long for a new spirit to enter into him — giving him the capacity to know God, and to relate to Him. The response of the Lord came swiftly. The inveterate liar, the impossible fraud, the uncontrollable egotist — Alves Reis — began to be transformed in a wonderful way by his encounter with God. Almost overnight he became a different man, ruled by entirely different passions and standards.

Even solitary confinement now became a place of peace and power. 'In the oppressive silence my spirit was asphyxiated, whilst dormant fleshly lusts and passions were aroused. The only solace was to fall on my knees and seek help from the One of Whom Paul the prisoner said, *I can do all things through Christ Who strengthens me.*'

Influenced by the great change which came over Reis, one of his confederates in prison (Adriano Silva) also began to seek God, and eventually became a convinced Christian. Then, as the result of many letters and visits to his cell, Reis's wife and eldest son came under the influence of his changed life, to experience for themselves the power and love of

Christ. As time went by, the former criminal became a trusted prisoner who was allowed to work freely as a 'missionary' among the hundreds of convicts. His wide popularity led to him being made stockkeeper and treasurer of the prisoners' canteen. While in prison he applied his literary flair to the revising of Portuguese tracts, and contributed regularly to a Christian magazine.

Alves Reis became a free man again in 1945, after serving 19½ years in prison. In one respect his release represented a loss to him, for he bade farewell to nearly two decades as 'chaplain' and evangelist to the needy souls of Portugal's criminal fraternity. He lived for ten more years after his release, becoming a well-known and much loved lay-preacher among the dozen or so evangelical churches in the Lisbon area, where his wife and married sons were settled.

Soon after his release he was often approached with projects by criminals who could not accept that he had been converted to Christ. They felt sure this must be an elaborate 'front', behind which he continued to operate fraudulent schemes. Within months of his release he was even offered a well-paid job by a bank, on condition he abandoned his preaching activities.

When Alves Reis died in 1955 he had no wealth in this world, nor did he care for it. He even requested that he should be placed in his coffin in a sheet so that his suit could be given to his eldest son. Nevertheless, he approached death as a sublimely happy man, for he knew that his Saviour had washed away all his sin, and his eye was now fixed on the wonders of the next life; on reunion with his wife Maria who had preceded him there, and on seeing the Lord Who had loved him and saved him.

The Story of 'Fiddler Joss'
Joshua Poole

HOWEVER TOUGH THE law, or however sophisticated the medical treatment, human ingenuity has never been able to find a sure remedy for the devastating problems of alcoholism and drug addiction. Yet the Christian Gospel has led to countless hopeless and notorious victims being utterly transformed and rehabilitated to live strong and constructive lives.

Perhaps one of the most dramatic examples of people raised from the depths of degradation and cruelty is that of the Victorian pub entertainer 'Fiddler Joss', who wrecked his family and his health, and yet became one of the best-known preachers of the 'evangelical awakening' which swept across Britain from 1859.

Joshua Poole grew up in a very poor Yorkshire home and his outstanding intelligence won him a scholarship to Skipton Grammar School. That was in 1830 — a tremendous achievement in those days. But he was a restless, unstable boy, and within three years he left school and went with his brother to live at Durham. There they stayed with an uncle who persuaded them to work in the mines and offered to look after their wages. They found jobs in pits where the tunnels were seldom more than 26-28 inches high and often a quarter of a mile long. They had to crawl about dragging 3-cwt loads of coal behind them, and according to a Royal Commission investigating at the time, boys like Joss and his brother worked shifts of up to 36 hours.

The Davy Lamp had been invented twenty-five years before, but few miners used it. Candles were much brighter, resulting in more work and more money, but explosions — and other accidents — were very common. After a long while as 'working animals' the brothers found that their uncle had swindled them by spending their money, and they went back to Skipton in disgust. Joss found work and learned to play the violin. Then when almost twenty years old, he threw up his job and joined a friend making a living as a travelling pub entertainer.

They made a lot of money playing in bars and fairs, but as they earned it, they drank it, and then they would walk the streets for days without food or work. Joss Poole became increasingly addicted to drink, and when he returned to his home town he was already beyond help. He fell in love with a quiet girl named Jane and at twenty-two he married her. She gave birth to a baby girl, but Poole treated them very badly and made no effort to support them. He invariably went home drunk, and even when Jane fell victim to tuberculosis he was never sober to nurse, help or comfort her. She died one night in utter loneliness, her husband in bed beside her in a drunken stupor. She died heartbroken and half-starved; her last effort in this life being the knitting of her own burial shroud.

Poole was penniless, so his father paid for Jane's funeral and said to his son, 'Come to my home, only

Home in a cellar

give up drinking and fiddling.' Joss was cut to the heart by his conscience, and when he lost his baby daughter only a week later he desperately wanted to start life again in a new way. But his feelings of remorse soon passed, and his good intentions with them. Then, within weeks of his wife's death he made up his mind to marry his sister-in-law, Mary.

At first, Mary was far from being keen on the idea. He was always drunk and she knew only too well how he had treated Jane. But as she saw more of him she began to feel sorry for him, until after a while she grew to love him, and convinced herself that she could change him. She was a girl who sincerely believed in God and in the Bible, and her principles told her that she should see the change before she married. Nevertheless, they were married after an engagement of only two months. During the first week Poole was a model husband. Then he launched himself into his pub life as never before. Frequently he was so drunk that he could not find his way home, and then he slept out in haystacks, barns, yards, and even pigsties.

One winter a serious illness brought him to his knees to pray for mercy and forgiveness from God, but as he recovered, he forgot it all and returned to his favourite haunt. The landlord welcomed him and the news spread that Joss was back with his fiddle. The house filled, celebrations commenced, and it was far into the night when he returned to Mary rolling drunk. From that day he was scarcely ever sober for seven years.

Mary gave birth to a boy, but Poole hardly knew. His ageing father (in whose house he still lived) could stand no more. One night as Poole lurched drunkenly into the house, the old man confronted him for a final show-down. In a violent temper, Poole punched him to the ground shouting threats of murder. His sister jumped between them and Poole turned on her like an enraged beast. Neighbours, roused by the screams, rushed in and overpowered him, and the following morning his father put him out of the house. So he took Mary and their little son, rented a cellar twelve steps below street level, and called it their 'home'. It was damp, dark and dirty, and Poole had little difficulty in turning it into a little hell.

He became indescribably cruel to his family, hardly ever providing for them. By the time his second boy

The fiddler in action

was born, almost the only thing which could touch Poole's heart was the sound of his children crying for food. While he played, dined and drank, his wife begged in the street. One night he committed such an act of violence that all his goods (such as they were) had to be pawned to pay for the damage. With the home so bare that there was only sacking for beds, his four-year-old boy became desperately ill, and they realised he was about to die.

Years later Poole said, 'To this day, the memory of Tommy's dying moments makes me tremble. My wife ran for the doctor who said, "There is no hope; he will shortly die." I had begun to say there was no God, no Heaven, no devil, no eternity and no punishment at all. I seized hold of Tommy and I put him on my knee. I said, "Let me hear you say you prayers." He put up his hands and prayed, after which he said, "Daddy, will you go with me?" ' Poole was moved to trembling, but when his other son died just two months later, there was still no bed in the cellar, no food and no fire. Mary buried her two sons in paupers' coffins and finally returned to the nightmare-cellar where she would never hear their voices again.

These were moments of intense sorrow and tragedy, when Poole would become sensitive to the suffering which he caused. But no human feeling or influence could prevent him from falling back into the life of sin and cruelty. Mary gave birth to two girls before the climax of horror came. Poole, as the result of his drunkenness, sustained regular delirium tremens fits. Mary had to destroy anything sharp for fear of murder, and spend nights on the pavement with a child beneath each arm. The time came when even Mary could stand it no longer and deserted him for the 'security' of the local workhouse, numbering herself and her two girls with the unwanted and destitute. But it was no protection. Poole was enraged. He found her and claimed her with vengeance in his heart.

He attacked her — but for the last time, for he was stopped by the police, arrested, and sent for trial. The magistrates bound him over on payment of two sureties, but no one would go surety for Joshua Poole, and so he was committed to Wakefield Prison for six months and led away friendless, watched by his bereft and destitute wife.

Poole entered the great gates of Wakefield to experiences which would never leave his memory. How well he would remember his first fit as he sat in a reception room. 'The scenes and haunts of my life rose up in the gloom of the place. Card playing, domino playing were visible in every corner. A confused crowd of strolling fiddlers and fallen girls danced and screamed around me, with all kinds of reptiles hissing and throwing out their venomous fangs and trying to coil themselves round my body, and in the background, there hung the very blackness and darkness of hell.'

At a quarter-to-six on his first morning the prison bell rang and the cell door was opened. Poole was assigned to work as a cook and moved to the cooks' cells. 'We slept ten in a room, the gas burned all night and the prisoners used to sit up nearly all night indulging in the most filthy conversation.' Soon, Poole had his first encounter with Mr Seth Tait, a prison officer, who asked him if he had ever been to Sunday School as a child. Poole, surprised by such a question, said that he had. Officer Tait began to speak to him about his wayward life and about his soul, but

Committed to Wakefield

Poole was in no mood to listen. 'For the first nine weeks, I was consumed by a burning desire for revenge on Mary. I laid a plan to murder her and the children, closing with my own death at my own hand.' Seth Tait, warder and self-appointed 'evangelist', did not give up, and spoke with Joss at every opportunity.

'From these conversations, when alone, I began to think of former days, especially the days of my boyhood. In my cell, I was nearly driven mad by the memory of my past sins, but the kindness of the officer increased. One evening, after having made my hammock, I was pacing my cell and my eyes fell upon a Bible lying on a table. I turned to it and began reading the 51st Psalm. *Have mercy upon me, O God, according to thy lovingkindness: according unto the multitude of thy tender mercies blot out my transgressions . . .*

'As I was reading it, my legs trembled beneath me and I shook from head to foot. The more I read, the worse I felt. I tried to kneel and pray, but it was no use. The devil came upon me and said, "It's no use; father and mother forsake you . . . wife and children have left you . . . it's no use praying." All that day and night I felt as though my heart would break. The next morning, Mr Tait began speaking to me and pointing me to Jesus.'

Here was the man who could not be reformed by anyone or anything. But now, the power of God was at work within him and for the first time in his life, he felt the full weight of his sins and uncleanness in God's sight.

'My soul's agony for three days was almost more than I could bear. On the fourth day, Mr Tait was writing in his office, and seeing my face bathed in tears, he looked at me, saying,

Have you not succeeded yet, Try, try again.
Mercy's door is open set, Try, try again.

'Before he had finished the verse I found peace and entered my cell that night resting by faith in Christ as my Saviour. All night I prayed, I sang and shouted for joy. The man in the next cell heard me singing and praying and although he had not prayed since his childhood, he prayed that night. The next day, I began telling the cooks about Jesus. Some of them laughed, others jeered, but others came to me by themselves and opened their hearts to me.'

Poole wrote to his wife, who had gone to her mother's home. He told her that he had become converted and was now a believer in the Lord Jesus Christ. With breathless anxiety, he waited for a reply. It came.

'You converted! No, never. You are only acting the hypocrite to get me back and to turn me out as you did before. As for me and my children, we never intend to live with you any more.'

When the day for his release came, Poole was met by his father and went to work for him, longing to make a fresh start. He found the strength, never possessed before, to resist all temptations to revisit old haunts and to slake his thirst. He also joined a Wesleyan Chapel, feeding his eager soul on the Bible teaching and on the friendship and encouragement of a band of people who had also experienced a personal conversion to Christ. One thing only was missing. 'In my heart,' he said, 'there was the void of being separated from Mary whom I had so much injured, and from my children. Earnestly, I prayed to God to bring about a lasting union.'

Seven months after his release from Wakefield it was so evident that Joss had been radically changed by a power outside himself, that Mary and the children overcame their fears, and the family was reunited. They moved back to Bradford where Joss set up a worthy home for them.

Quite early in his 'new' life Joss became deeply concerned for youngsters who were heading into the kind of life which he had left behind, and he decided to open a home Bible class in an attempt to influence them. He started by opening his Bradford house on Sunday mornings to seventeen-year-old rowdies. Inside six months his class registered forty-two members, and was named — the School for Bradford Roughs.

Poole never missed an opportunity of explaining to people how he had become a Christian and how the power of God had saved him from sin, misery and self-destruction. He began to accept invitations to speak in chapels and public meetings, and wherever he spoke people crowded in to hear 'Fiddler Joss', the ex-drunkard. By the time he was thirty-eight, he was speaking at so many meetings that he gave up his job, having been strongly urged to do so by several of the leading preachers of the day. His first large meetings as a 'popular' preacher were at Leeds where he preached to thousands of people in specially convened public meetings.

Joss Poole's main task, however, was speaking to the lost classes of society — alcoholics, the destitute, tramps and street prostitutes. He travelled the country with other well-known evangelists, and while they took the larger public meetings, he and his wife Mary would conduct meetings in the most degraded parts of towns and cities, often into the early hours of the

Joshua Poole

morning. Over the years many thousands of people were affected by his testimony and persuasive appeals to turn to the Saviour. In all parts of Britain souls moved by Joss Poole's tearful pleas came to trust in his Lord, and found their way into the memberships of churches.

Joss never drank again. He sorrowed often and

deeply about his early cruelties, and dedicated his life to the deliverance of others from 'the twin tyrants of unbelief and alcohol'. He lived very simply and inexpensively, gaining a well-deserved reputation for his consistent lifestyle and his relentless effort in the harvest of lost and precious souls.

'Fiddler Joss', one of the outstanding preachers of a hundred years ago, stands in the long line of souls for whom society could do nothing at all. He ruined his life and destroyed those nearest and dearest to him, but the unparalleled mercy of God found him and worked in his heart until he cried, *Hide thy face from my sins, and blot out all mine iniquities.* Then God heard him, forgave him, and utterly transformed him.

Leader of the Lords
Viscount Alexander
of Hillsborough

LORD ALEXANDER OF Hillsborough occupied a very prominent place in the political life of Britain for many years. Through five years of the Second World War he ruled the navy as First Lord of the Admiralty in Churchill's coalition Cabinet. After the war he became the first Minister of Defence, and later served an unusually long period as Leader of the Opposition in the House of Lords.

Alexander was an earnest, blunt, hard-working politician, noted for his determination when in office, and for his outspoken contributions to debates. 'But,' said the Lord Chancellor at his death, 'there can be no dispute that the dominant feature of his life was his Christian faith and belief.'

Albert Alexander was born in 1885 at Weston-super-Mare. He was still a baby when his father died leaving a wife of twenty-eight, three other children and no money. His mother started work in a corset making business, and Alexander later recalled, 'Throughout my childhood I never remember her leaving home on a working day after a-quarter-to-eight in the morning or getting home much before half-past-nine at night, and usually she brought work home with her even then.'

In those days the elementary schooling provided
for poorer children was completed at thirteen years of
age. On the morning of his thirteenth birthday,
Alexander was preparing to go looking for work
when his mother handed him the weekly fee of seven
pence and told him to go and enrol at the secondary
school. But he knew only too well that the fee would
come from his mother's sacrifice of some basic essential, and so he found himself a job as an office boy.
Instead of secondary school he went to evening
classes, and succeeded in preparing himself for the
same public examinations as the better off regular
schoolboys.

Alexander was twenty-two when he began to think
very seriously about his relationship with God. He
had been brought up to attend church — playing
football for a local church team — but his churchgoing did not really mean anything to him. It was
merely outward religion. Then he began to attend
another church in the town where the preacher
challenged his hearers to seek a living relationship
with the Lord. It was there, following a talk with the
minister in his vestry, that Alexander first believed in
the Lord Jesus Christ as the only One Who could
forgive sinners, and he prayed to God for pardon and
real conversion. The minister later wrote to him
during the First World War saying, 'You know how I
cherish you for that Sunday evening in my vestry long
ago! I love every memory of your usefulness since.
May you win through to the crown of life.'

Alexander recalled this experience in the House of
Lords, when he told the peers: 'I was brought up in
the Church of England and was in it until the age of
twenty-two. Indeed, I should have been in it now if I

The House of Lords

had not discovered a bigger and wider truth. That is: that you cannot live on family, traditional religion. If you want salvation, you need to be born again. You have to go to the life-giving Word of God: the Word made flesh.'

Soon after this experience of personal conversion Alexander married, and together the young couple sought to serve Christ in their lives. Although he was afflicted with a nervous stammer he was persuaded to speak at mid-week Bible Study meetings at his church, and eventually went out lay-preaching. In time he completely overcame his speaking difficulty and took on the work of lay pastoring a small chapel outside Weston-super-Mare.

Alexander rose quickly to the post of Clerk to the Education Committee of the Somerset County Council, still continuing spare-time studies for further promotion. But at this point, his hold on his faith began to waver as he formed ideas about life and people which were to seize all his passion and enthusiasm for many years. He admired greatly the strenuous social activities of the Co-operative movement, seeing in the movement a tremendous potential for putting right social evils. Although he had been a fervent and sincere preacher of the need of conversion for every sinner, he now came to think that the main purpose of Christianity was simply to make the world a better place to live in. He began to see the church, not as a mission to the *souls* of lost people, but as a God-given model of service to humanity.

Alexander now felt that God wanted him to be a modern William Wilberforce — a great social reformer — but he did not appreciate the vital difference between his new attitude and that of the historic reformer. Wilberforce had vigorously committed himself to social improvement, but he never lost sight of the fact that Christianity is following Christ. He always remained anxious and ready to rescue the souls of individual people and to bring them to a personal knowledge of Christ. He never forgot that this is a doomed world and that the greatest need of human beings is to be reconciled to God before they die. The young Alexander was no Wilberforce. When he committed himself to social reform, his Saviour, tragically, became less important to him.

After the First World War — during which Alexander rose from the rank of private to captain — he took a post as a full-time trade union officer in Somerset, where he spent two years negotiating better working conditions for local government officers. Then, through his schoolgirl daughter, he stumbled across the opportunity of a lifetime. His daughter was due to take a scholarship examination, and so Alexander encouraged her with the promise, 'If you win this scholarship, I tell you what we'll do: we'll all go up to London for a fortnight's holiday to celebrate.'

She won the scholarship, and the family went to London. While there, Alexander heard that the Co-operative Society was looking for a Parliamentary Secretary. It would be for him a considerable step forward and would mean a move to London. He applied, and won the appointment against stiff competition from a large number of well-qualified applicants.

The day came when Sir Thomas Allen, Chairman of the Co-operative Congress, walked into the office and said, 'Here's a job for you. I want you to defeat the Lloyd-George government.' A new method of taxing company profits was passing through Parliament which threatened to eat into Co-op dividends. Alex-

ander went to work persuading MPs to oppose the
measures, touring the country for meetings, and
mounting as effective a campaign as he could to
preserve the 'rights' of the Co-op. Against seemingly
impossible odds, his campaigns killed the offending
proposals. Sir Thomas Allen called him into his office,
looked at him with raised eyebrows, and gave
unusually warm congratulations. He had never really
expected success. 'Young man,' he said, 'you had
better go into Parliament.' When Sir Thomas
pronounced, it was invariably done, and so, in 1922,
Albert Alexander duly stood as Co-operative candi-
date for the Hillsborough constituency of Sheffield
and was elected to Parliament.

The family now lived in Twickenham and were
enthusiastic supporters of a church where the so-
called 'social gospel' was preached. The teaching was
that if only people would live in brotherly kindness
towards each other the world would gradually become a better place, and the 'kingdom of God' would
be accomplished. The teaching of the Bible, that the
human race has fallen from God's favour and cannot
achieve such conduct, had been placed on one side.
The biblical insistence that people need forgiveness
and new life from God, was regarded as outmoded
and irrelevant. Alexander became convinced more
firmly than ever that his duty was to improve the
conditions of people by social welfare and political
legislation. His view was that a better world would
make a better people, and he said so in public
meetings, and in articles written on behalf of the
Brotherhood Movement and carried by the popular
press.

Many people in Parliament at that time regarded
Alexander as no more than a Co-op representative. It

Alexander as First Lord of the Admiralty
with King George VI

was probably to keep the Co-operative movement
happy that he was made First Lord of the Admiralty
in the 1929 Labour Government. Whatever the motives behind his appointment, he came to be regarded
as one of the outstanding successes of that particular
Cabinet. Suddenly everyone realised his ability. But
after two years he lost office and his parliamentary

seat in the landslide defeat of the Government in 1931. He had to wait four years before he was returned to the Commons, and then he steadily moved to greater honours.

In the early stages of the Second World War Winston Churchill left his post as First Lord of the Admiralty to take over the helm as Prime Minister. Because the navy had been Churchill's chief interest it weighed heavily upon him to appoint a strong and capable man to follow him at the Admiralty. Without hesitation and with complete confidence Churchill appointed Albert Alexander, who remained First Lord to the end of the war.

In many ways, the war was a cruel blow to Alexander's confused and optimistic philosophy of life. The ugliness of war exposed fallen human nature. It showed just what the human heart was capable of, and how hopeless was the policy of reforming human behaviour by means of education, prosperity and legislation. However necessary and laudable these things, they were powerless to change sinful hearts and improve sinful behaviour. As he reflected on the ugliness of war, Alexander found himself thinking — as he used to do years before — that a personal relationship with God was the burning need of millions of people, and their social and bodily needs paled into insignificance beside that need.

One of Alexander's responsibilities at the Admiralty was to appoint a new Astronomer Royal. He selected his man — a Cambridge professor — sent for him, and offered him the appointment. The professor asked for a week in which to think it over. When Alexander saw him again he declined the highest honour of his profession because after much prayer to God he felt he should continue to devote his leisure time to Christian work among university students. Alexander was deeply moved. He left his office that day and went home very thoughtful and greatly affected. This man had room in his life for the *souls* of others. As for Alexander, he had left that behind in his earliest days as a lay-preacher.

Gradually he found his way back to the faith of his early life, and resumed regular reading of the Bible. He had never ceased to believe in the Christ, to Whom he had given his life at the age of twenty-two, but he had put modern human ideas about religion before the teaching of God's Word, and so had missed the real experience of a close walk with God. Alexander came back to the point where he recognised that the only hope for a soul was the sacrificial death of Christ, and a personal experience of conversion.

How would the kingdom of God come? His years of public life had at last taught him that it would not come by political measures, and a few years later he frequently would say so when speaking to large audiences. The kingdom of God was an eternal domain which could only be entered in this life by coming to personal faith in the Saviour.

After the war, Alexander became the first Minister of Defence, a new office, coming under heavy fire at one point for a double change of mind about whether National Service should be 12 months or 18 months. Then, after five years in that office, he was created a viscount and went to the House of Lords.

In 1955, Alexander, aged seventy, was unanimously elected Leader of the Opposition in the Lords. His activity was impressive for a man of his years. Firstly, there was a full programme of affairs to lead in the Lords. Then he would often be found on the platform of public meetings — especially Protestant meetings.

He opened churches, spoke at office Christian Union meetings, and sometimes preached.

The minister of the local church which Viscount Alexander attended said, 'It was our privilege here to know Lord Alexander as a Christian man. He and her ladyship became members of our church in June 1956 and I think it is true to say that Lord Alexander loved this little place of worship. We shall sorely miss him; for his membership was expressed in practical terms, and every Sunday morning, if he was in residence on the Island, would see him in his place in church, whatever the weather, and toward the end, however ill he was feeling. I said to him once, "My Lord, you are an example to men half your age." "Ah!" he replied. "You see, I have been forgiven so much."'

On May 10th 1961, a historic debate took place in the Lords on the issue of Church unity. While many peers expressed the view that the attainment of a single, united church, unencumbered with a doctrinal basis, was the most important objective for christendom, Lord Alexander argued that such an aim showed a complete misunderstanding of the Christian faith. Not all who took the name Christian were *true* Christians, he insisted, for being a true Christian depended on what a person believed.

Lord Alexander's words stand on the record of the Lords: 'If you look at the fifth chapter of John's Gospel, verse 39, you find that the Master says, *Search the Scriptures: for in them ye think ye have eternal life.* There is no other place to search for eternal life but here. Jesus never said, "What saith the Sanhedrin, or the high priests, or the archbishops or bishops, or the Pope?" but, *What saith the Scriptures?*'

Alexander firmly believed that some professing

churches could not really be classified as 'Christian' at all, because they did not take their religion from Christ and the Scriptures.

'I believe,' he said to the Lords, 'that you can find salvation only through the Word of Life and what it says in the Bible — I take you to the way of salvation *...I am the way, the truth, and the life: no man cometh unto the Father, but by me.'*

No greater tribute could be paid to the latter years of Viscount Alexander than that spoken by a peer who did not share his spiritual convictions. Lord Longford said, 'He based his life on the Bible. He knew it through and through, as no other layman in the House could perhaps claim to know it. Daily he strove, by prayer and scrutiny of conscience, to carry out the will of God as he understood it. He pursued that end as ardently in his last years as I imagined in the days when he was a young preacher — perhaps even more so...he pursued it with a conviction, a candour and commitment that were the visible source of his strength...'

Viscount Alexander of Hillsborough passed from this world into the eternal kingdom of God in January 1965, having proved over the years that the Bible alone has the remedy for the human predicament, and that Christ Jesus alone can change the human heart.

Sailor, Deserter, Slave-Trader
John Newton

JOHN NEWTON WAS THE only son of a sea captain who owned a small fleet of private trading vessels. Captain Newton planned a rugged upbringing for John. He would go to school not a day longer than was necessary, then he would go straight to sea, visiting ports and meeting people of all nationalities. John's mother had died when he was seven, but not before she had stored his young mind with a good knowledge of Bible teaching. After her death he was sent to boarding school until his father's plan came into operation. John was then taken away from school to be given his first taste of life at sea, in a vessel trading round Mediterranean ports.

He entered into the life with relish and soon picked up the ways and language of the seamen. Frequently he went to extremes of coarse behaviour, but when the voyage was over he returned home feeling sickened and ashamed of himself. Pangs of conscience, however, were soon brushed aside, and weeks spent on dry land made him bored, moody and frustrated. His father soon found a space for him on another ship, and life became worth living once again. Voyage followed voyage, and on each one his conduct became more abandoned and his conscience more hardened.

Once, when he was home, John arranged to meet some friends to look over a warship anchored in the harbour. He arrived at the quayside too late to meet his friends, and spotted them in a small boat which was taking visitors to the warship. His disappointment suddenly turned to horror as the small boat capsized, drowning all his friends. The tragedy haunted him for weeks, bringing home to him the reality of death, and stirring within him a fear of ever meeting God with a guilty conscience. In later years he reflected, 'I often saw religion as a means of escaping hell, but I loved sin and was unwilling to leave it.'

When he was still fifteen, John went into a highly religious phase, in which he meditated and prayed every day, became a vegetarian and fasted twice every week. For two years he regretted his former conduct and tried to make amends by abstaining from all normal enjoyments. All the time he thought he had the ability to earn God's forgiveness, but he later said that this proud idea made him 'gloomy, stupid, unsociable, and useless'. It certainly did not bring him into touch with God in any meaningful way, and when he gave up his self-infused discipline he quickly went to the other extreme of moral abandon.

At seventeen, John's father saw that he was becoming more moody than ever and arranged for him to go on an unusually long voyage. Before going, John was given three days to carry out some business for his father in Deal, Kent. In the house where he lodged he met Mary Catlett, a girl who immediately became the idol of his life. The three days became three weeks and John returned home to face the fury of his father for having missed his ship. What was to be done with the boy now? Captain Newton's only answer was another voyage, but to the lovesick John the voyage seemed to last for years, and as soon as he returned, he made straight for Mary. Again he frustrated the plans of his father by overstaying his visit. Captain Newton lost his patience — he even thought of disowning his son — but then, out of the blue, disaster struck, but in a way which Captain Newton secretly welcomed.

Young Newton was roaming the streets wearing his seaman's check shirt when he was spotted by a press-gang lieutenant of the Royal Navy. The navy desperately needed crews to fight the French fleet and John Newton became one of those who were ruthlessly press-ganged aboard a man-of-war, the *Harwich*. On hearing the news, Captain Newton made no effort to claim his son, but instead sent a note to the captain of the *Harwich* recommending him for a midshipman's rank. This gave Newton many privileges, but he resented his enlistment and despised his appointment.

The *Harwich* set sail and took up station in the English Channel waiting for the rest of the fleet to assemble. Newton was given a day's leave ashore. He spent three days with Mary at Deal and returned to suffer the discipline of the Royal Navy. The fleet left Spithead in January 1745 and immediately ran into a freak southwesterly gale. Many ships were driven on to the Cornish coast, while others, including the *Harwich*, fled for the shelter of Plymouth harbour.

Somehow Newton heard that his father was in Torbay — about twenty miles away. If only they could speak together he was sure that he could persuade his father to give him a permanent position in his Mediterranean trading fleet. Newton had been warned once against desertion, but how else could he reach his father? The opportunity came when he was put in charge of a landing party with orders to watch out for possible deserters. He made a break for it himself and followed the road to Torbay. He was just outside Torbay when he was stopped and interrogated by a group of soldiers, who put him in irons and marched him back to Plymouth.

On board the *Harwich*, a humiliating punishment awaited Newton. A gathering of the whole ship's company was called, and in the presence of them all Newton was stripped, whipped, and degraded to the lowest rank. His midshipmen friends were then forbidden to speak to him.

Newton became indescribably depressed. His back was cut to ribbons; he had no friends to speak to, and he was made to do the dirtiest jobs aboard ship. Worst of all he had little or no hope of ever seeing Mary again, for the fleet was leaving Plymouth for five years service in the East Indies. There was nothing left to live for, and in his bitterness Newton began to blame God for his predicament.

Life among the press-ganged seamen of the 'lower deck' was cruel, coarse and crude. After a period of suicidal depression Newton adapted to his environment. He won general approval by acting the young tearaway, retailing filthy and blasphemous jokes to humour the admiration of all. In fact, he lived for the pleasure of being regarded as the instigator of everything obscene.

After some time, the fleet called in at Madeira for stores. On the last morning of their stay Newton heard that the commodore of the fleet had ordered the *Harwich* to exchange two of its crew for two men from a ship bound for Sierra Leone. He immediately pleaded to be allowed to transfer ships, and within half an hour was discharged from the navy and installed in the new vessel. Newton's conduct on joining this private vessel became worse than ever, as he subsequently recorded: 'From that time on I became totally corrupt. Not only did I sin, but I got others to sin with me.' Newton was insolent and lazy in his work, incurring the intense dislike of his captain.

A man named Clow, who was a part-owner of the new ship, was aboard travelling as a passenger. Clow owned a plantation in Sierra Leone where he also bought slaves for resale. It was obvious to Newton that slave-trading paid Clow very well, and he decided to cultivate a friendship with him, and to try to get work with him. When the vessel arrived at Sierra Leone he went ashore, a penniless but optimistic recruit to the slave-trade.

Newton settled with Clow on the largest of three islands known as the Plantanes, just two miles off the Sierra Leone coastline where the River Sherbro meets the sea. He had high hopes of doing well for his new employer, but within days of their arrival Newton went down with malaria. Clow set off on an expedition leaving Newton in the hands of his negro mistress, who for some reason had taken an instant dislike to him and decided to abandon him to the fever. Delirious and unable to move, he was left out in the torturing sun to die. But the woman had underestimated his strength, and after a few weeks he began to show signs of recovery. Starved and semiconscious, he attempted to walk, and groups of slaves were incited to jeer at him and mimic his staggering movements.

To keep alive he had to crawl to the plantation at the dead of night to unearth and eat raw root vegetables. Somehow he recovered his strength, and when the opportunity came, he sent a letter appealing to his father for help.

When Clow returned Newton complained bitterly about his treatment, but Clow would not believe him. For a while matters improved as Newton did his utmost to please Clow on a trading voyage, but then another trader convinced Clow that Newton stole from him and swindled him whenever his back was turned. As it happened dishonesty was about the only vice Newton could not be charged with, but Clow grew intensely suspicious from that moment. Clow's resentment rapidly fanned into hatred, and this found many outlets.

For long months he would subject Newton to endless victimisation, denying him food and clothing. Newton recalled: 'My clothes were threadbare. What clothes they were! I had a shirt, a pair of trousers, a cotton handkerchief instead of a cap, and about two yards of cotton to wrap around me. With no more than that I have been exposed to up to forty hours of incessant rains and gales, without the least shelter, when my master was on shore. I developed violent pains . . . I used to creep out at night to wash my shirt on the rocks, and put it on wet so that it would dry while I slept. When a ship's boat came to the island I would hide in the trees, ashamed to be seen by strangers. And yet . . . my conduct, my principles, and my heart were still darker than my outward condition.'

After about a year under Clow's cruel domination — and several more letters home — Clow allowed him to leave and join another trader on the same island. Overnight, his fortunes changed. Newton's new employer trusted him, and rewarded his efforts with a highly comfortable lifestyle. Soon he posted him to help manage one of his factories on the coast of the mainland.

Back in England, Captain Newton had received one of his son's letters and had arranged for a trading ship named *The Greyhound* to call at Clow's settlement to collect him. Help was on the way.

The Greyhound had a crew of about thirty and traded at most of the settlements along the West African coast. When the captain put ashore for Newton at the Benanoes (islands near to the Plantanes) he was told that he had moved a great way inland, and so all idea of collecting him was abandoned. The vessel was about a hundred miles further along the coast when the ship's watch reported a smoke signal from the shore. Such signals usually indicated that trading was invited, so *The Greyhound* dropped anchor and discovered Newton and a friend. They had signalled the passing vessel — an unusual event at that point of the coastline — in the hope of obtaining some long-needed personal supplies.

Newton, now aged twenty-one, was no longer so interested in returning home. His new employment gave him scope for an easy life free from moral inhibitions. But the captain of *The Greyhound* told him a false story of a great legacy awaiting him at home, and this, together with his memories of Mary, enticed him on board.

Newton was welcomed aboard as a passenger and gentleman and settled down to a life of comfort. *The Greyhound* was due to continue trading for another year before heading for home — up to 1,000 miles further from England than the coast of Sierra Leone. The only useful thing Newton had to do was to master and learn by heart *Euclid*. 'Except for that,' he

Leisure aboard a man-of-war

recorded, 'my life was one of continual godlessness and profanity. I do not know that I have ever met a man with a mouth more vile than my own.'

Newton channelled his behaviour and thinking even further into the exploration of debased humour and conversation. He 'preached' from the ship's

Bible, twisting the text into vile stories. Eventually hardened seamen found his talk sickening, and the ship's captain began to dislike him intensely, regarding him as a Jonah who would bring disaster to the ship. He would promote drinking contests to see which crew member could hold his liquor best.

As soon as *The Greyhound* finished its trading calls, after a few days at Annabona (400 miles west of Gabon), they put out to open sea to return home. Keeping to trade winds they had a 7,000 mile voyage before them.

First they sailed due west, near to the coast of Brazil, then they turned northward to Newfoundland, where they stopped to take on fish. They left, heading east for home, on March 1st, 1748. Newton, who was now an experienced and hardened seaman, was very uneasy about the state of the vessel. After a long expedition in a tropical zone, she was badly in need of repair. The sails and rigging in particular were in no fit state to withstand stormy weather. On March 9th Newton happened to pick up and read a religious book, but he soon pushed it aside, and 'went to bed that night feeling as indifferent to God as I had ever been'. Suddenly he was startled out of his sleep by the force of a violent storm. Pounding waves drove the raging sea below deck so that water poured into the cabin where he lay. He climbed to the upper deck to find mountainous waves crashing across the vessel. 'I'll man the pumps,' shouted Newton. 'No,' yelled the captain, 'fetch me a knife from below.' Turning to obey, Newton saw the man at the pumps swept overboard by another gigantic wave. If he had done as he intended he would have been lost.

One side of the ship was almost entirely battered to pieces and water flooded in so rapidly that it could not be pumped out. It amazed everyone that the ship remained afloat. The terrified and despondent crew were convinced that the end had come, and the captain cursed Newton — their 'Jonah' — for ever having come aboard. At first Newton seemed impervious to danger and rallied the spirits of the crew. But gradually, lashed to the deck for safety, and working the pumps, he began to realise the staggering reality of the situation. It was surely impossible for *The Greyhound* to ride any more of these colossal waves. He turned to look at the flooded area of the ship which he had been pumping. 'If that won't do,' he said, 'the Lord have mercy upon us.' Suddenly, for the first time in years, his blasphemous words seemed to bite back at him. 'What mercy do I deserve?' he thought. The answer was painfully obvious.

The colour drained from his face and his mocking, arrogant manner gave way to deep fear and clamouring thoughts. 'Is there a God?' he began to ask. 'Is there life after death?' The very thought of death seemed to confirm that there was. His instincts warned him to prepare himself to meet his Maker, the very thing which frightened him most. How could he face the God Whom he had insulted for so long? He began to feel a crushing despair.

He was moved from the pumps to take a turn wrestling with the helm and as he did so, his thoughts raced feverishly over all that he knew about God. Scripture passages read years before now came to his mind with startling clarity. 'I now began to think of that Lord Jesus Whom I had so often ridiculed. I remembered the details of His life and death, a death for the punishment of sins not His own, but for the sake of all those who should put their trust in Him. How could I trust Him to bear my punishment? I really wanted proof that God could do this. I wished that these things were true.'

Expecting to die at any moment, Newton now prayed desperately to God for help and safety. The answer to his frantic prayers was to come more quickly than he could have expected. As daylight came the fury of the storm diminished and the back-breaking work of operating the pumps seemed to be having some effect. The damaged side of the vessel was crudely patched with planks and sealed with blankets. Then it was Newton's turn for some rest. But how could he rest? Seizing a Bible, he went into his cabin and read these words of Christ:– *And I say unto you, Ask, and it shall be given you; seek, and ye shall find; knock, and it shall be opened unto you. For every one that asketh receiveth; and he that seeketh findeth; and to him that knocketh it shall be opened. If a son shall ask bread of any of you that is a father, will he give him a stone? . . . If ye then, being evil, know how to give good gifts unto your children: how much more shall your heavenly Father give the Holy Spirit to them that ask him?*

Under threat of death, Newton thought more clearly than ever before. 'Upon this I reasoned — if the Bible is true as a whole, then this particular passage must be true. The writer, if he is God, has promised to give the Spirit to all who ask for it. Therefore I must ask for it. And if I am given it, then I must trust the whole Bible as God's Word.'

With his mind grappling with spiritual problems, one other thing worried him. He could see that God could forgive sinners, but would that include him? In everyday life, one can forgive a friend, but to forgive your arch-enemy is impossible. Why should he expect God to do this? The answer lay in the Bible, where

Newton read about Saul of Tarsus, a man who hated Christ and persecuted Christians; yet Saul was freely forgiven, renamed Paul, and called by God to be an apostle. If there was mercy for Saul, thought Newton, surely there could be mercy for him too.

Newton found other passages in the Bible which challenged his heart. He read the parable of the barren fig tree in *Luke 13*, and saw that when the useless tree was condemned to be cut down by its owner, then the keeper pleaded for the tree to be given one more chance to bear fruit. Newton grasped the Lord's meaning in the parable — that there would be mercy for repenting sinners regardless of their past lives.

Another parable which gave him great encouragement to go to Christ in prayer for mercy and new life was the parable of the prodigal son in *Luke 15*. 'I felt that no one more perfectly fitted the picture of the prodigal than I did. The goodness of the father in not only receiving, but in running to meet such a son — an illustration of the Lord's goodness to returning sinners — deeply moved me.'

The furious storm had given way to a gentle breeze, but not before rendering them helpless. The ship was unseaworthy and they had no clear knowledge of their position. Every man aboard knew that the slightest change in the wind would be enough to send them all to the bottom. The damaged side of the ship had to be turned constantly to face the wind in order to keep the vessel leaning in the opposite direction. At all costs the broken side had to be kept out of the water. An approximate course was set, and they prepared for the perilous journey back to England.

Day after day, the men manned the pumps to keep down the water constantly seeping into the stricken hull. They tried to satisfy their hunger on rationed portions of salted cod, the only food each day being half a fish divided among twelve crew members. All their bread, livestock and spare clothing had been washed overboard, and as the temperature dropped to near freezing point they began to feel the effects of exposure and starvation. As the days passed, they grew too weak and emaciated to operate the pumps and one seaman died. The day came when the food ran out, followed soon after by the water, and every-thing seemed lost at last. Only the pain of exhaustion tempered the misery and despair that now gripped every mind. But that very day — exactly four weeks after the great storm broke upon them — the battered *Greyhound* sighted a small island off Lough Swilly, on the north coast of Ireland, and the next day they reached port, knowing they had survived the impossible.

'About that time,' wrote Newton, 'I began to know that there is a God Who hears and answers prayer. I felt a peace and satisfaction on that day which I had never known before.'

How different was the man who emerged from that terrible voyage. Newton, like Saul of Tarsus, had met the Lord and given his life to Him. Clothed with a new humility and character, all his inner motives and desires were changed. Newton stepped off the gang-plank of the half-wrecked *Greyhound* as a man with a new life within, and a new start ahead of him. He had come to life in a spiritual way. In the words of Christ he had been 'born again'.

Although Newton continued to sail with — and command — slave ships for seven more years, in time he came to be one of the most implacable opponents of slavery. It was Newton who more than anyone else inspired and encouraged William Wilberforce in his

John Newton

campaign to abolish slavery. He married Mary Catlett, an earnest Christian believer whom he had loved
since his early youth, and longed to devote himself to
the Lord Who had forgiven his sins and granted him a
new life. For some years he held the post of Tide
Surveyor at Liverpool, serving also as lay pastor in a
local independent church. He caught up on a missed
classical education, and was in due course appointed
curate of Olney Parish Church in Bedfordshire.

Newton drew large numbers of people to his
preaching, started one of the first Sunday schools in
the country, and wrote some of the finest and best-
known hymns in the English language, including
*Glorious things of thee are spoken, Zion, city of our
God; How sweet the name of Jesus sounds in a
believer's ear;* and, *Amazing grace! How sweet the
sound, that saved a wretch like me.* Together with his
close companion the poet William Cowper, who also

lived at Olney, he compiled a hymnbook — *The Olney Hymn Book* — from which scores of hymns are still in use today. One of these great 'Olney' hymns fits perfectly Newton's own approach to the Lord while on board *The Greyhound*:–

> *Approach, my soul, the mercy-seat*
> *   Where Jesus answers prayer;*
> *There humbly fall before His feet,*
> *   For none can perish there!*
>
> *Thy promise is my only plea,*
> *   With this I venture nigh;*
> *Thou callest burdened souls to Thee,*
> *   And such, O Lord, am I.*
>
> *Bowed down beneath a load of sin,*
> *   By Satan sorely pressed:*
> *By war without, and fears within,*
> *   I come to Thee for rest.*
>
> *Oh, wondrous love! to bleed and die,*
> *   To bear the cross and shame,*
> *That guilty sinners, such as I,*
> *   Might plead Thy gracious name.*
>
> *'Poor tempest-tossèd soul, be still,*
> *   My promised grace receive:'*
> *'Tis Jesus speaks — I must, I will,*
> *   I can, I do believe.*

After sixteen years at Olney, Newton was appointed to the united parishes of St Mary Woolnoth, and St Mary Lombard Street, in the City of London. Here, in a pulpit of great influence, he ministered for 27 years. He was certainly one of the greatest preachers of his day, being the confidant and counsellor of some of the most powerful political figures, and a campaigning reformer whose influence was felt in all the momentous social advances of his time. He was also one of the greatest letter writers of his age. One of his volumes of letters entitled *Cardiphonia* (or 'letters to the heart') has been republished many times down to the present day, exemplifying the highest literary order of letter writing, and the most profound and tender spiritual advice.

John Newton preached the good news of forgiveness and conversion as a gift from God to all who sincerely repent, and he preached it with characteristic vigour and urgency until he was past eighty years of age. When advised to stop preaching for the sake of his health, Newton replied, 'Shall the old African blasphemer stop while he can speak?'

In his will, Newton penned these words:– 'I commit my soul to my gracious God and Saviour, Who mercifully spared and preserved me when I was an apostate, a blasphemer, and an infidel, and delivered me from that state of misery on the coast of Africa into which my obstinate wickedness had plunged me ... I rely with humble confidence upon the atonement and mediation of the Lord Jesus Christ, God and Man ... as the only foundation whereupon a sinner can build his hope, trusting that He will guard and guide me through the uncertain remainder of my life, and that He will then admit me into His presence in His heavenly kingdom.'

No sketch of the life of John Newton can possibly leave out the words which he ordered to be used on his own gravestone:–

'Once an infidel and libertine, a servant of slaves in Africa, was, by the rich mercy of our Lord and Saviour, Jesus Christ, preserved, restored, pardoned, and appointed to preach the faith he had long laboured to destroy.'

The Man Behind
the Red Cross
Jean Henri Dunant

THE STORY OF JEAN HENRI Dunant is without doubt one of the most extraordinary that can be found. It is the story of a man who was at the same time one of the greatest failures and one of the greatest successes of recent history. It is the story of a man who dined with kings, and ate scraps with tramps; the story of a hard-headed and self-seeking man of the world, who yet revealed more conscience and feeling than any other influential figure of his time.

The fast-moving adventure of this man's seemingly contradictory life spanned the glamour and gore of a changing Europe from 1828 to 1910. Dunant spent his boyhood amidst the sumptuous surroundings of wealthy Geneva, in Switzerland. His family possessed both riches and social status, his father being a land-owning city councillor. His parents were also devout churchgoers, and Dunant, a broad-shouldered, red-headed, seventeen-year-old was soon searching out the answers to spiritual questions for himself. What was a Christian? How could a person know God? What was the purpose of life?

A dynamic evangelical preacher had stirred Geneva to the heart since being appointed a pastor in the city

Dunant in retirement (left), and at thirty-five

in 1816. He was Pastor Louis Gaussen, who preached
Sunday after Sunday in a large church, packed to the
doors. There, in the crowded pews, young Henri
Dunant listened regularly to sermons pressing the
need for a personal conversion to Christ and he
became deeply affected. By the time he was eighteen,
he had become a praying Christian whose life and
future was surrendered to Christ.

Dunant lost no time in finding ways of spreading
his new-found faith to others. Every Sunday at two
o'clock he would pass through the grim iron doors of
the city prison to visit prisoners in their cells, and to
speak to them about how he had found the Saviour.
For his student friends, he organised weekly rambles
over the hills, the main topic of conversation being the
need to find the Lord. Before long these rambles were
attracting over a hundred young people. Always they
were rounded off by a meeting held in Dunant's
house where, amidst the white pillars and dark panel-
ling of his father's great reception hall, many of his
friends found the way to God.

This meeting grew into the first YMCA in Switzerland, and in due time the parent of many others, for as
members moved away to work or study in other parts
of Europe, they started similar meetings for young
people. Dunant, who became a travelling bank executive, was able to keep in touch with all these
offshoots, and hold them together. So full of drive
was he as organiser of these many meetings, that a
fellow worker wrote, 'My task has not been an easy
one. I had Dunant to restrain — he has amazing zeal
and energy. It was he who knew how to tie the
threads that broke, to rally the backsliders, stimulate
those who weakened, and warm the fainthearted.' As
a young Christian, Dunant had virtually become the

founder and mainspring of the European YMCA.

His organising and diplomatic skill was also noticed by his company, who promoted him to represent their interests in North Africa. Then, when he was twenty-six, they made him the general manager of all their investments in Algeria. Here, as the regional head of a major international bank, Dunant found himself in a new and challenging country, once run by fanatical tribesmen, but now brought into subjection by France. His chief task was to organise the development of mines, factories, homes and farms in estates covering 50,000 acres.

Dunant's life had been spent amongst wealth, but the wealth of Geneva did not pamper its owners. Personal spending was always restricted, and self-indulgence or extravagance frowned upon on principle. In French-conquered Algeria, however, wealth meant luxury, status, power and vast possessions. A conflict broke out in Dunant's mind as he dreamed of wealth, and at the same time tried to honour his Lord and live for Him. He continued to visit his European YMCA meetings and to live more or less as a Bible-believing Christian, but he began to think that there could be no harm in indulging his ambitions for greater wealth to just a small degree.

Although it was in breach of his conditions of employment, Dunant tried a little speculative business of his own, buying land and selling it at a profit. Then he went further and secured from the government a lease of over a thousand acres of ground to develop plantation, mining and factory interests. His 'small step' cost him his job as general manager of the Genevan banking company, and he was plunged headlong into seeking his fortune as a private speculator in Algeria. Gradually he now became consumed

The battle of Solferino, from a painting by Horace Vernet

by his ambition and desire for success and wealth, and his heart grew cold towards God. His memories of youth faded into the background and he devoted all his mental powers to building a business.

While a banking executive Dunant had moved in very high circles. He knew many rich and influential people, including such powerful figures as General de Beaufort, the Chief of Staff of Napoleon III. From his numerous contacts he was able to secure many thousands of francs to invest in the development of his Algerian estates — investments on which he would pay a 10 per cent annual return. He hastily constructed the most modern mills, built homes and laid out plantations, anticipating that he would soon get the necessary planning permission for access to water supplies. But neither his diplomacy nor his influential connections could hurry the French Algerian authorities into granting the water rights he so desperately needed. Without water, the estates could not even begin, but investors still had to be paid interest.

After a year of frustration and delay, Dunant was reduced to desperation. Having tried almost everything to secure water, there remained only one course of action open to him: he would petition the emperor, Napoleon III of France. At that time, Napoleon had decided to help Italy regain territory which had been occupied by the Austrians. The French and Italian alliance began the first 'modern' war, utilising railways and morse telegraphy. Also for the first time war correspondents followed the conflict, sending dramatic despatches back to their newspapers.

The fighting began on Italian soil with the French gaining rapid victories over Austrian forces. Dunant made up his mind to secure an audience with Napoleon III while he commanded his troops in Italy. To wait for the emperor to return home would mean certain bankruptcy. Dunant's plan was to cultivate the goodwill of the emperor by presenting a book he had written about him — a book overflowing with flattery for Napoleon's international achievements and aims. Then he would grasp his opportunity to explain how his Algerian estates were wasting away because of local government indolence in granting planning permission for water.

Dunant arrived at the front line and sought out his friend, General de Beaufort, who gave him directions to Napoleon's headquarters. A great encounter was about to take place at Solferino, near Brescia, where Napoleon was positioned with 150,000 men and 400 cannon. Secure in the hills were the troops of Emperor Francis Joseph of Austria, 170,000 men supported by 500 cannon. They occupied the fortified heights of Solferino. Altogether, over 300,000 men faced each other along a ten mile front.

Dunant arrived on the fringe of the battlefield by daybreak on 24th June 1859. At 6 am, Austrian foot soldiers began to advance towards the French line, hordes of white-coated men, their giant standards bearing the Imperial Eagle. Bugles and drums sounded, and the massive French line also began to move, the armour of lancers and dragoons catching the early sun.

To Dunant, it seemed like a game — puffs of white smoke — crackling of muskets — and thousands of colourful uniforms. But suddenly it developed into the most terrible bloodbath as men charged at each other, bayonets extended, thrusting, lunging, cutting and stabbing. Men fell in their hundreds, both from hand-to-hand fighting, and from the barrage of musket and cannon fire sweeping down from the hills.

When the foot soldiers reached deadlock, then the cavalry were ordered in, galloping over the strewn and writhing bodies, followed by gun-carriages, crushing and killing countless wounded men. Wave after wave of Frenchmen vainly attempted to storm the fortified hills held by the Austrians, until a fearful thunderstorm broke, and then, under cover of this cloudburst, they swarmed through the cordon of cannon into the town of Solferino.

So the Austrian line was broken and their retreat began. Even Napoleon was stunned and appalled at the cost of his victory as he surveyed the battlefield, seated on his immaculate stallion. From the perimeter of it all, Dunant was experiencing a state of utter shock. He wrote:

'When the sun rose on the twenty-fifth, it disclosed the most dreadful sights imaginable. Bodies of men and horses covered the battlefield; corpses were strewn over roads, ditches, ravines, thickets and fields; the approaches of Solferino were literally thick with dead. It took three days and three nights to bury the dead on the battlefield ... the bodies were piled by the hundred in great common graves.'

The wounded on the battlefield, at least forty thousand of them, lay their heads in muddy, blood-stained puddles to drink — young men whose expectations of victory and glory lay shattered with them. Dunant made his way to nearby Castiglione, expecting to find Napoleon's HQ. Instead, he found hundreds of gravely wounded soldiers of both armies piled in churches and on the pavements. Napoleon had moved on. There was food, water and lint available, but the peasants were panic-stricken and there were no doctors to attend the wounded.

For three days and three nights, Dunant lived out

the nightmare he was to remember all his life, organising and leading the medical relief work among the dead and dying of the Battle of Solferino. He became known as 'the man in white', being revered almost as an angel. With a few peasant helpers he fed the men and dressed their wounds until eventually a handful of doctors arrived to set up a field hospital.

On the fourth day Dunant found a cart and set off to locate the emperor. He still had to save his Algerian business empire, and to do so he had to see Napoleon. Napoleon, however, could not be located anywhere, nor were his aides in the least helpful. Yet suddenly Dunant hardly cared. He was so deeply affected by the experience of Solferino and his three days with the thousands of wounded men that he stumbled about like a man in a stupor. Nothing — not even his mounting business worries — could get Solferino out of his mind.

Eventually, he sat down and poured his memories out on paper to produce a book which shocked the world and moved even heads of state. It was 'Souvenir de Solferino', in which he recounted in detail the horrors of the battle and its aftermath, and in which he called for relief societies whose aim would be to provide care for the wounded while being regarded as neutral by both sides on the battlefield. Immediate practical support for Dunant's idea came from a group of prominent men in his native Geneva. A retired general, a distinguished lawyer and two doctors joined him to form a committee of five who would bring the idea into reality.

They invited heads of government to send representatives to a conference. Dunant, meanwhile, went to a Berlin conference to get support for his scheme. In Berlin the idea of neutral relief workers

A scene from 'The Man in White', produced by Films du Jeudi, Paris

mushroomed out to include neutral recognition for the injured as well. Dunant was given an audience by the King of Saxony, and won the approval of almost everyone. He visited several European heads of state, and then presided at the first international conference in Geneva for the promotion of the Red Cross relief organisation and the formulation of the Geneva Convention. The persuasiveness and diplomacy of Dunant carried sixteen governments, of which fourteen sent delegates to the conference.

But as Dunant travelled round Europe promoting the Red Cross his troubles in Algeria loomed larger and larger. Once again, Dunant pinned everything on his hero — Napoleon III. If only he could get an audience he was sure that his troubles would be resolved. Napoleon was due to make a state visit to Algeria and so Dunant made sure he was officially invited to be presented to him. The day came when Dunant, who had ready access to the sovereigns of Europe, at last stood before the elusive French emperor. He told him about the Red Cross, and then he told him about his business problems due to the absence of water on his estates. To his immense relief and delight the emperor promised to help, and Dunant went his way as if walking on air. Full of optimism, he went in for further investments and developments. Napoleon, however, did nothing whatever to help him.

Then came plague and war in Algeria, followed by cholera, locusts, earthquakes, drought and the most terrible winter ever recorded. Dunant's estates were tottering on the very brink of ruin. The business empire for which he had abandoned his God was about to collapse. He shut his eyes in blind hope and turned back to preoccupy himself with the Red Cross, which was about to receive its first real test as a credible organisation.

In Prussia the notorious Bismarck had cast his sinister shadow across the international scene. Dominating the king, he forced a terrible and unnecessary war with Austria in which two armies of a quarter-of-a-million men clashed. The Prussians were equipped with new breech-loading rifles which enabled them to rapidly crush the Austrian army, killing 25,000 men. Amidst the bloodbath the conflicting armies observed the Geneva Convention for the first time. Prussian Red Cross teams were able to clear all their wounded from the battlefield in safety. The Austrians had no Red Cross organisation with the result that their wounded men lay in the open throughout two days and nights of heavy rain until Prussian relief workers found them. It was at the same time a triumph for the Red Cross and a bitter indictment of governments which refused to make provision for their wounded.

When Dunant was honoured at a banquet thrown by the Berlin royal household, they did not know that his financial collapse was about to take place. Inevitably his largest bank overdraft was called in, so that other investors began to ask for their money back. Dunant lost everything — his property, plantations, mills, oak forests, lead and gold mines, and his family fortune. In Geneva, nothing was more disgraceful than bankruptcy, so that Dunant, living in Paris, dared not return home. To his fellow leaders in the International Red Cross he became such an embarrassment that they were obliged to deprive him of his office.

Until this point, life for Dunant had amounted to flights of genius, when his brilliant ideas coupled with exceptional planning and negotiating skills secured all the rewards of international recognition. His Red Cross organisation would leave an indelible mark on world history. Yet in the midst of success and triumph he had always teetered on the edge of a precipice of doom and destruction. The fear and shadow of business collapse had permeated even the moments of highest achievement and applause. After his financial crash there were fewer and smaller opportunities for brilliance. A surviving small income kept him respectable, while from time to time international flare-ups summoned him out of oblivion to organise local Red Cross activities, but the stigma of failure limited even these opportunities of usefulness.

During the great war between France and Prussia — when Bismarck humiliated and routed Napoleon III — Dunant made a dramatic undercover escape from besieged Paris in order to initiate diplomatic discussions with the Germans. Apart from such brief moments of glory, Dunant was a spent man. At one point he came to England in search of a new career, but finding no door of opportunity open to him he was glad to accept a job trying to sell a newly-invented gas-operated organ.

Back in Paris, at only fifty-three years of age, he was forced to join the ranks of the destitute. He had no money, no relatives or friends, and frequently could not even pay for a night's common lodging. He spent long, dreary days trudging round the cold Paris streets — haunted by his memories and his disastrous financial humiliation. Jean Henri Dunant had finally fallen to the very bottom of human society. He had abandoned the God of his youth and directed his trust to the gods of this present life. He had switched his allegiance and desire to the forces of materialism — riches and status. He had placed his trust in his own ingenuity and abilities, and staked all on the word of an emperor. But when he looked to this vain world to keep its promises, it betrayed his trust, and threw him down to oblivion.

Now, rejected by the world and shunned by his friends, Dunant's hopes eventually turned back to the Friend Who had once said, *I will never leave thee, nor forsake thee.* Far away from the scenes of earthly success and failure, he went back to His Lord and Saviour, pleading for forgiveness and a renewed sense of spiritual life and peace. He laid the sins of his self-seeking life at the Cross of Calvary, believing with all his heart that His Saviour had there borne the punishment and penalty on his behalf.

Dunant's prayer was that of King David's — recorded in *Psalm 25* — *Remember not the sins of my youth, nor my transgressions: according to thy mercy remember thou me for thy goodness' sake, O Lord.* And as he yielded his life once more to Christ, he found again the reality of walking with God and knowing Him. The prodigal had returned.

Dunant was an old man when he was rediscovered by the world. Suddenly the schoolmaster of a small town in the Swiss Alps realised that the lovable patriarch with a long white beard living in the local pensioners' hospital was the long-lost founder of the Red Cross. A Swiss journalist came to investigate, and the story was soon headline news around the world. Immediately, there was great acclamation, culminating in the award to Dunant of the first Nobel Prize. His rediscovery and his Nobel prize doubtless meant a great deal to him, but it was nothing by comparison to his rediscovery of Christ and the prize of knowing Him.

Dawn Breaks over Europe
Martin Luther

MARTIN LUTHER, BORN in 1483, grew up amidst the peasants and poverty of a small mining town in fifteenth-century Germany. His father was a wood-cutter who later became the manager of a small foundry, smelting iron. He was a hardworking man, but a formidable father who imposed the most rigid discipline on his sons.

In those days school was a place where knowledge was driven into boys by fear of punishment. It was closely bound up with the Catholic Church, and young Martin Luther was well and truly indoctrin-ated in the fear of God and the power of the Pope. He once said that whenever he heard the name of Christ as a child he turned pale with fright, imagining a terrible judge Who would one day dominate eternity.

Martin was fourteen when he went away to high school at Magdeburg, but as there was not enough money to keep him he joined the ranks of the poor students who begged in the streets for their living. However, he was one of the fortunate ones, because one day wealthy Frau Ursula Cotta took pity on him and welcomed him into her home. Luther was such an exceptional student that he was urged to go on with further studies, so at the age of eighteen he set off for the most famous place of learning in Germany, the University of Erfurt. With his father now better off financially, Luther could afford to take a room and support himself at Erfurt. He studied so hard that by the age of twenty-two, he had achieved the degrees of Master of Arts and Doctor of Philosophy.

Luther's academic triumphs, however, could not suppress a fear which had come to worry him: 'What about my soul? Where is God? What takes place in eternity?' When one of his closest friends was murdered, the thought came back with even greater force: 'What would happen to me if I were suddenly called away without warning?'

Luther soon assumed the status and privileges of a lecturer at the university, conscious of the admiration and pride of his parents. How excessively they demonstrated that pride when he spent his first holiday with them as 'Doctor Luther'! They had no inkling that their pride and satisfaction was about to be shattered, and their son's career thrown away, all in the panic of a few moments.

It happened while Luther was walking the last stage of his return journey to Erfurt. Quite suddenly, he became enveloped in a tremendous thunderstorm. As the rain poured down, Luther moved slowly on until a blinding bolt of lightning seared through the sky and struck the ground immediately ahead of him. He fell to the ground, certain that his end had come. Terrified, he shouted, 'Help! Beloved Saint Anne, help! and I will immediately become a monk.' A peal of thunder passed away and Luther, still shaking, rose to his feet. He was stunned, surprised to be alive, and more agitated than ever before about his standing in the sight of his Maker. He felt there was no other course open to him than to keep his vow and to enter a monastery. He was about to submit himself to be bound by the very chains of superstition and man-made religion which years later he was to shatter at the beginning of the Reformation of Europe.

It was a very pale and shaken Luther who returned to Erfurt. He promptly invited all his friends to a final supper-party at his room and broke the news that he was going into a monastery. All pleaded with him to change his mind, but nothing would persuade him, and as soon as the party was cleared away and his friends had dispersed, Luther set out — at the dead of night — to apply for admission to the Augustinian Order monastery in Erfurt.

'I thought God was not concerned about me and if I got to Heaven, it would depend mostly upon me. I knew no better than to think that by my own accomplishments, I must rid myself of sin...so I became a monk and came in for a most bitter experience at the same time. Oh, I thought that if I went into the monastery cloisters to serve God in a cowl, with head shorn, He would reward me and bid me welcome.'

Luther, was twenty-two when he said goodbye to the world, returned his degree gown to the university, and wrote to inform his horrified parents that he had become a monk.

His first lesson at the monastery was designed to make him humble. He was assigned to cleaning, fetching and carrying, and other simple jobs, and after the day's work was completed, he was sent into the town to beg for food. Luther accepted it all as an essential part of his training, and in return he looked to the tranquillity of the monastery and the companionship of holy men to help him attain peace of mind.

The Wartburg Castle, near Eisenbach,
where Luther translated the Bible

He was soon to be bitterly disappointed.

The more he tried to live a holy life, the more he realised how utterly impossible it was. The cloister certainly removed him from the temptation of the world outside, but not from the countless sinful thoughts of his own mind. Was there, he wondered, any cure for his preoccupation with himself, or for constant thoughts of pride, envy, lust and hostility? Was there any way of being cut loose from lying, grumbling, complaining, gossiping, resenting, and all the other unholy things which well up from within oneself?

The more Luther looked to other monks for help and example, the more dejected he grew at their shallow lives and empty chatter. Nevertheless, he took absolutely seriously all the monastic remedies for sinful thoughts — even to the extent of inflicting punishment and torture on himself in an effort to be 'purified'. Several times he rendered himself unconscious through pain, but no matter how rigorously he performed the prescribed self-punishing acts, he could not improve himself or banish his impure thoughts or selfish desires.

The day came when the Erfurt monastery was visited by Johann von Staupitz — Doctor of Divinity, founder of the University of Wittenberg, and Vicar General of all the Augustinian monasteries in Germany. As Staupitz walked round the cloisters there was one young monk he could not help noticing, and that was Luther. He was painfully conspicuous. His sunken eyes and wasted frame betrayed his lack of sleep and constant fasting, while his dejected expression revealed that he had failed to find any spiritual peace as a monk. Having inquired for Luther's name, Staupitz spoke to him.

'Why are you so sad, brother Martin?' he asked.

'Oh,' replied Luther, 'I don't know what will become of me...it is useless that I make vows to God; sin is still the strongest thing in me.'

'Oh, my friend,' said Staupitz, 'over a thousand times I have vowed to God to live righteously and I have never kept my vows. Now I make no more promises for I know I cannot keep them. If God will not show me mercy for the sake of Christ, I shall never stand before Him. If you want to be converted, do not be eager to learn about all this self-denial and discipline and all these tortures — love Him who first loved you.'

This was certainly a new thought for Luther. He had approached religion entirely to get some form of personal spiritual comfort and peace — being willing even to punish himself mercilessly to get it — but he had not started with God. He had always thought of God as a remote creator, a hard taskmaster and a harsh judge, but now he had a new starting point in his search for God — he must trust Him as a God of love. However, it was no more than a starting point, because he still thought that he had to earn his salvation by doing all the things which the Church demanded.

Luther had spent two years as a monk in the dark cloisters of the monastery when he was made a priest. Much of the time he created a diversion from his confused feelings by devoting himself to considerable study. In a damp, dark cell lit by a shaft of light from a small window-opening and with a candle flickering over his parchments, Luther grappled with the Greek and Hebrew texts of the Bible. Staupitz directed him in the study of the Bible, particularly the New Testament epistles *Romans* and *Galatians*. But while he excelled in the technical analysis of the text, he did not yet grasp the simple meaning of their message, that sinful people cannot earn their forgiveness, but must receive it as a free gift from God. To Luther, salvation must be worked for and deserved.

Staupitz, discovering the latent genius in Luther, took a special and paternal interest in him, and arranged with the ruler of Saxony for Luther to become Professor of Philosophy at Wittenberg University. There he taught classes, continued his

Luther's Bible translation and work desk

own studies, and lived in a cell in a small Augustinian cloister.

At the age of twenty-six Luther was called upon to make a journey which transformed his opinions. He was selected by a group of monasteries to represent their interests in a visit to the Pope at Rome. Luther grasped at the opportunity for he imagined that Rome was the very heart of godliness — the centre of the Holy Church. He felt sure that he would derive new and vital spiritual light and experience from the visit, and he set out on the southward journey across the Alps with very great — if somewhat naive — anticipation.

On his way he was stunned by the wealth of some of the monasteries he visited, and by the hypocrisy of so many of the monks. But he was to be more amazed by Rome itself. Luther entered Rome like a wide-eyed schoolboy, drinking in all the superstition and ceremonial, believing all that he was told, and eagerly participating in the services and ritual. But he soon found that the priests of Rome laughed at his serious-ness and sincerity. He was sickened by the indifferent way they raced through their liturgical services. The more he spoke to priests, bishops and other dignitar-ies in Rome, whether in private or over the dinner table, the more he discovered hypocrisy and frivolity coupled with appalling ignorance of, and irreverence for, the things of God.

Above all, he found that the city which was the centre of the 'Holy Church' had the worst crime rate of any place he had set foot in, despite its great number of priests and churches. 'No one can imagine the sins and scandalous crimes committed in Rome,' he wrote. 'The city is filled with chaos and murder.' Luther had never for one moment suspected the things which he saw, but Rome demolished in one stroke all his naivety and superstitious belief. He had given his life to the Roman Catholic Church because the Church claimed the power to forgive sins and save souls. But he found that at the centre and metropolis of the Holy Roman Empire, the proud claims of the Church amounted to nothing. She was powerless to influence even her own prelates and priests in the direction of true godliness.

This realisation of the weakness and inadequacy of the Roman Church had a profound effect upon Luther because the *Church* was his only hope for salvation. Although he had become a monk, passed the theological examinations and been made a priest, he had no personal assurance that his sins were forgiven, and no awareness that he was in touch with God. None of the penances, services, chanting or fasting had helped one bit. His only hope had been to pin everything in blind trust on the power of the Holy Church. He reasoned that if the Holy Church said these things were the way to God, then it *must* be right.

The fatal visit to Rome at last shattered his unswerving trust in all the pronouncements and prescriptions of Rome. If the Church could not be revered and respected, then neither could her pronouncements. Luther promptly lost confidence in her pomp and ceremony, and not surprisingly, when he returned to Wittenberg he was more anxious than ever to understand what the Bible had to say about true religion and the way to find God.

Staupitz, who was at a loss to know how to help Luther through his spiritual struggle, pressed him to study for the degree of Doctor of Theology in order that he might devote himself to teaching the Bible. Luther set himself to the task and achieved the degree within two years. Then, aged twenty-eight, he was posted to the young university at Wittenberg to serve as professor of the Bible.

As Luther searched the New Testament for answers to his many questions about the true way to find God, he noticed that the only people who thought themselves able to earn God's favour were the self-righteous scribes and Pharisees, and these were roundly condemned by the Lord Jesus Christ. He saw that, according to the Bible — *There is none righteous, no, not one . . . for all have sinned, and come short of the glory of God (Romans 3.10 and 23).*

Luther (second from left) with his fellow reformers

As he studied the *Psalms* in preparation for his lectures, he was struck by the terrible desolation and agony endured by Christ on the cross of Calvary — all foreshadowed in *Psalm 22* — and he realised that the only reason for such suffering was that Christ was bearing the punishment of human sin in order to make an atonement. He felt totally overwhelmed as he contemplated the immeasurable love of Christ, that He should come from Heaven into this world on such a costly errand of mercy to undeserving sinners. But how could any individual become sure that his or her own sins were forgiven? For a time this remained a great problem for Luther, until he proceeded to study and lecture on Paul's epistles to the *Romans* and *Galatians*. Here he discovered the meaning of conversion to Christ, and how God in that unmistakable experience enables people to know and to feel that their sins are forgiven, and that He has accepted them.

Luther was thirty years of age when he had this experience himself. He was sitting in his cell studying Paul's letter to the *Romans* when he came to these words: *The just shall live by faith (Romans 1.17).*

'My situation was that, although an impeccable monk, I stood before God as a sinner troubled in conscience, and I had no confidence that my character would satisfy Him. Night and day I pondered until I saw the link between the justice of God and the statement that *the just shall live by faith.* Then I grasped that the justice of God is the righteousness by which, through grace and sheer mercy, He justifies us through faith. Immediately I felt myself to have been reborn and to have gone through open doors into paradise. The entire Scripture took on a new meaning ...this passage of Paul became to me a gate of Heaven.'

Luther's discovery was that the blessings of forgiveness and a new life from God came as a free and gracious gift to all who believe in Christ's atoning sacrifice as the only way for the washing away of sin, and who place their trust and their lives in Christ alone for their salvation. Immediately Martin Luther felt certain that *his* sins were all forgiven, and that he was — by grace alone — a child of the living God, with a new heart and life. But how different was the teaching of Paul to that of the Church of Rome, which taught that acceptance with God is achieved on the basis of good works!

Immediately after his experience of conversion, Luther's name and fame spread as he preached and taught the Bible in churches and in monasteries as well as in his university. He became increasingly appalled at the avarice and hypocrisy of the Roman Catholic clergy, and the deceitful trickery of church leaders, of which Pope Julius II was among the most outrageous. His dissatisfaction was brought to a head in 1517 when monks from Rome began raising money for the building of St Peter's by 'selling' the Pope's pardon for sins — indulgences.

The experienced vendor of indulgences Johann Tetzel, a Dominican priest, went from town to town selling them in the most shameful manner. His sermon seldom varied, and usually concluded with these words:

'Consider this: that all who are contrite and make their contributions will receive complete remission of all their sins. And listen also to the voices of your dear dead relatives and friends imploring you and saying: "Pity us! Pity us! We suffer in dire torment from which you can redeem us for a mere pittance." Don't you want to help them? Hear your father or mother saying, "We bore you, fed you, left you our money, and now you are so heartless that you are not willing to set us free at such a small price. Will you let us die here in flames?" Think that you have the power to release them, because —

> *The moment the coin in the coffer rings*
> *The soul from purgatory springs.'*

On the eve of a great religious festival when great crowds gathered in the town, Luther nailed to the church door his response — the now famous 'Ninety-Five Theses' in which he denounced the sale of

The statues of Luther and Melanchthon in the town square, and the 'theses door' of the castle church, Wittenberg

indulgences and denied that the Pope could forgive sins.

By this time Luther had clearly formulated the three great principles of the Reformation: first, that sinners are justified (declared righteous) before God by faith alone, and not by their works; secondly, that every true believer has direct access to God without the need for the mediation of priests or church; thirdly, that the Bible is the *sole* authority for true religion, and the church is to submit to its teaching.

The struggle to break the fetters of superstitious, man-made religion had begun. By the time of his death twenty-nine years later, Luther had become the great Reformer whom God used to usher in the Reformation of Europe and to restore the faith of the Bible. By the enabling power of God he withstood all opposition and laboured as a preacher, teacher, writer, thinker, contender for the faith, translator of the Bible, and as a guide and counsellor to burgeoning Reformation churches in Europe. Through his ministry a countless host of people came to see the Lord's method of salvation — by grace alone, through faith in Christ.

His best-known words are probably those uttered at the end of his defence at the Diet of Worms in 1521, where he was condemned as a heretic and excommunicated from the Church of Rome. When called upon to repudiate his teaching, he declared: 'Unless I am convicted by Scripture and plain reason, I cannot accept the authority of popes and councils, for they have contradicted each other. My conscience is captive to the Word of God. I cannot and I will not recant anything, for to go against conscience is neither right nor safe. Here I stand, I can do no other, so help me God! Amen.'

Burned at the Stake
Bilney, Tyndale & Latimer

WHAT KIND OF COURAGE was it that made people willing to perish in the searing flames of martyrdom in the turbulent days of the English Reformation? What was the experience of faith that turned even cowards into heroes? This is the story of three very different men who died at the stake rather than deny their personal experience of the living God.

It was in 1517 that Martin Luther nailed to the door of the Castle Church, Wittenberg, the 'Ninety-Five Theses' which exposed the darkness and tyranny of the Roman Church and touched off the Reformation in Germany. At that time, the picturesque towns and green countryside of England lay under the rule of Henry VIII, while the nation's religion was increasingly dominated by Thomas Wolsey — cardinal archbishop of the Roman Catholic Church.

Wolsey was a priest with a burning ambition — twice frustrated — to be elected pope. He had climbed the ecclesiastical power ladder in a spectacular manner after being appointed a king's chaplain. At forty he became Archbishop of York, acquired (by political chicanery) a cardinal's hat within a year, and then took over the seals of the Lord Chancellor from the Archbishop of Canterbury to become, after the king, the most powerful man in both church and state. Wolsey was without doubt an arrogant and greedy ruler. Whenever he appeared in public he would be splendidly robed in scarlet velvet, with two priests carrying silver crosses walking in front of him. His palace staff numbered over 500 people, not including the army of agents and spies on his payroll. If he could not *yet* be pope, he certainly intended to live as a pope in England, and to preserve the power and the supremacy of the Roman Church.

In those days, if anyone failed to honour and obey a priest of Rome, he was liable to suffer the same fate as John Browne of Ashford, who was 'insolent' enough to contradict a priest by exposing his ignorance in public. Within a few weeks Browne was brutally dragged out of his house, thrown into prison, and burned alive as a heretic.

The teaching of Wolsey's Church amounted to nothing more than superstition, image worship, and empty ritual. It was a 'faith' which was imposed by force — on pain of burning — upon the whole nation, and there seemed no prospect of any change as the might of the civil government upheld the Church. Nevertheless, events began to occur which led in time to a dramatic turn of events. Supplies of a small book started to come into Britain and filter into the universities. It was the New Testament, produced by the Dutch scholar Erasmus, first in Greek and later also in a Latin edition.

Immediately the presence of these New Testaments provoked a storm of protest from the 'Holy Church'. The priests knew that such books would cause students to question and doubt the power and authority of the pope and bishops. In fact, the outlawed

Tyndale, in exile, translating the Scriptures

book did far more than this — it transformed in heart
and life large numbers of its readers.

At Cambridge in 1519 there was a short, slightly-
built student of about twenty-four named Thomas
Bilney, recently made a priest, and now studying
church law. He was a studious young man who took
his religion very seriously, believing that if he could
live up to God's commandments his soul would be
saved. The only trouble was — just like Luther some
years previously — he felt that he could not live up to
those standards. The more he tried, the more his
conscience showed him his faults and threw him into
despair, driving him to his fellow priests for help. He
would confess his sins to them, and they would
prescribe penances, but all this did nothing to make
Bilney feel that his sins were blotted out and forgiven
by God.

Soon he began to suspect his fellow priests as —
'wolves who seek nothing from their flock except
their milk, wool and hide . . . leaving their souls to the
devil.' Bilney spent all his money paying their penances, then gave up in despair and fell to doubting
whether there was a God of mercy at all. How he
longed to know the truth.

One morning as he walked up to a group of friends,
he heard them talking about Jesus Christ. Anxious to
know what they were discussing, he was surprised to
find they had secured copies of the Erasmus New
Testament which was causing so much trouble.
Thomas Bilney secretly bought himself a copy and
began to read. He later wrote: 'At the first reading I
well remember I fell by chance on this sentence of
Paul — the most comforting sentence to my soul —
This is a faithful saying and worthy of all acceptance,
that Christ Jesus came into the world to save sinners:

of whom I am chief.' Bilney felt as if his soul had been released from prison. 'This one sentence did so uplift my heart, which had previously been wounded with guilt and almost in despair, that immediately I felt a marvellous comfort and quietness, inasmuch as my bruised bones leapt for joy.' The thought that a *chief* sinner could be sure of being saved astonished him. And if this was so, surely he too could be saved.

He had always thought that the Church had the power to save souls by such means as the mass, priestly absolutions and penances, but according to his New Testament people were not saved by any mediating action of the Church or priests, but by the free gift of forgiveness available to any repentant sinner who applied in prayer directly to Christ. 'I see it all,' he said. 'My vigils, my fastings, my pilgrimages, my purchase of masses and indulgences, were destroying rather than saving me.'

Thomas Bilney turned to Christ in earnest, secret prayer that very day, asking that He would forgive and accept him. He realised that he was totally unable to earn the forgiveness of God by anything which he could do. He now grasped that he must depend on Christ to do everything necessary, and he believed with all his heart that Christ had taken the punishment for all his sins on Calvary's cross. He prayed that God would change his life and become real to him, and he yielded over his life to Him. The result was that he *felt* forgiven, and he *felt* that he had become a child of God. At last he knew that God was working in his life.

Bilney was the first of a group of Cambridge men who came to know God through reading His Word. Although by nature shy and reserved, he immediately began to speak to others about his discovery, and a

number of fellow priests met with him daily to study
the New Testament, some of whom were to become
martyrs for the sake of Christ. He then applied
himself to preaching in the towns and villages of East
Anglia the message of the Gospel — *repent and be
converted* — believing that God had called him to
'evangelise His people'.

In the rest of the country increasing numbers of
educated people were beginning to question the
teaching and authority of the Church as copies of
Luther's books came through the ports from Germany. Cardinal Wolsey was enraged. Breathing out
death-threats to anyone found in possession of these
'heretical' books he ordered a public bonfire for them
at St Paul's.

At Cambridge the new learning was becoming even
more infectious. Hugh Latimer was a contemporary
of Thomas Bilney. A wealthy farmer's son with a
powerful intellect and great force of character, he too
was a priest studying further divinity. But he was
absolutely set against the new religious views of
Bilney and others. Latimer still believed in the magic
and mystery of the Roman Church. Indeed, he used
to worry greatly at the mass for fear that he had not
mingled the wine and water well enough for it to turn
into the blood of Christ. It was more than he could
stand when some of the lecturers began to teach
the Scriptures straight from the Greek Testament.
In 1524, to mark the completion of his graduate
studies, Latimer was due to preach before the whole
assembled university. He chose as his subject the
denigration of Luther's colleague, Philip Melanchthon, putting all his passion into an attack on the
book of the German Reformation.

In the crowd of listeners stood Thomas Bilney. As

he watched Latimer, he saw a priest of the Church, devoted to its pomp and ceremony, yet at the same time he saw a man who in reality had no personal experience of the Lord God in his own life.

When the speech was over Bilney quietly approached Latimer and asked if he could speak with him. 'Bilney heard me at that time,' said Latimer, 'and perceived that I was zealous without knowledge; and he came to me afterwards in my study, and requested me, for God's sake, to hear his testimony. I did so — and to say the truth, by his words I learned more than before in many years...from that time forward I began to savour the Word of God, and forsook the school doctors and such fooleries.'

In the quietness of Hugh Latimer's study, Bilney had told him how he had found forgiveness of sins, and how people could come to know God personally in the simple way described in the Bible. 'Master Bilney was the instrument by which God called me to knowledge...for I was as obstinate a papist as anyone in England.'

Hugh Latimer underwent an experience of conversion in the true biblical sense: *If any man be in Christ, he is a new creature; old things are passed away; behold, all things are become new.* He dropped his old ways and joined Bilney in spreading the faith of the Bible. He became a preacher of great power and many people came to know God through his preaching in the university and town of Cambridge.

The opponents of the Reformation observed with mounting apprehension the great crowds of people flocking into the churches whenever Latimer, Bilney, and their friends preached, and they began to plan ways of silencing them. The diocesan bishop was urged to deal with them as heretics, but when he swooped on a church one evening to hear Latimer's heresies at first hand, the young preacher changed his subject and foiled his persecutor. Within a year, however, persecution began in earnest. One of Bilney's collaborators had preached a Christmas Eve sermon in which he condemned the evil ways of the bishops. Within two months he was arrested, taken to London, and threatened with burning. The iron hand of the Church was now raised against these Bible-believing priests and academics. Soon, however, a new vehicle would be spreading the Word of God into the homes of ordinary people. This was the English translation of the New Testament from the pen of William Tyndale.

Tyndale, a former student at both Oxford and Cambridge, had undergone the same conversion experience as Bilney and Latimer soon after being consecrated a priest. Subsequently he had gone to live at Little Sodbury Manor, the stately home of Sir John Walsh in Gloucestershire, to be governor to his children. Tyndale found that whenever he tried to explain the biblical way of salvation to people, the monks and priests resisted him for all they were worth by spreading lies and rumours to discredit him and his message. 'I perceived by bitter experience,' he wrote, 'that it was impossible to establish the lay people in any truth except the Scriptures were plainly laid before their eyes in their mother tongue.' On one occasion Tyndale exclaimed to a haughty priest who derided the Bible — 'If God spares my life, before many years I will cause the boy that drives the plough to know more of the Scripture than you.'

Let the people be deceived no longer by the Church, thought Tyndale; they must see the Word of God for themselves. Sir John and his family shared

Henry VIII with Cardinal Wolsey

Tyndale's understanding of the Bible and encouraged him in his translation efforts, but soon opposition grew to such a pitch, that he had to pack his few belongings and move to London. He hoped to secure the protection of the Bishop of London, who was not yet so openly antagonistic to the Reformation as he later became. But Tyndale's hopes proved to be naive, for he found the bishop altogether unsympathetic.

Though Tyndale gained a good friend and suppor-

ter in a wealthy London merchant named Humphrey
Monmouth, he realised that it would be suicidal to
translate the Scriptures anywhere in England, and so
in 1524 he sailed to Hamburg, never to set foot in his
native land again. On arrival, he travelled through
Germany and called upon Luther, who warmly welcomed him and gave him a place where he could carry
out his great work. In one year, the translation was
ready for the printer, the only hindrance being that
most printers were located in countries where it was
illegal to print Bibles. Tyndale's first attempt to print
in Cologne was discovered by the authorities. He had
to escape with as much as he could carry and flee to
Worms, where the first copies were at last successfully
printed.

Just when the authorities in England were arresting
the Bible-preaching clergy, no less than 6,000 English
Testaments were smuggled into England by Humphrey Monmouth, collaborating with continental
merchants. Soon, Bilney and Latimer were seized and
sent to stand trial before Cardinal Wolsey. On this
first occasion they were not condemned. In fact,
Latimer was given freedom to preach all over England. But the warning shot had been fired, and the
Bible men were commanded to teach strictly in
accordance with the practices of Rome.

As Tyndale's Testaments streamed into the country, the authorities grew still more alarmed. Anyone
caught in possession of a copy faced the death of a
heretic, and at St Paul's, a massive public bonfire was
made from hundreds of confiscated copies. When
investigating agents uncovered the secret distribution
network for these New Testaments, the young men
and women responsible had to flee abroad to save
their lives. Ultimately Henry VIII — at the instigation

of Wolsey — issued orders to British foreign agents to track down Tyndale and put him to death.

The pace of events quickened further when in 1527 Bilney, who had continued preaching from the Bible, was arrested on the orders of Wolsey. Through desperately cold November nights he lay in a damp cell, awaiting trial for heresy. The Bishop of London, his appointed prosecutor and judge, tried hard to save him from death by persuading him to renounce his errors. 'Submit to the authority of the Church,' he pleaded, 'and affirm that God speaks only through her.' Bilney, however, was determined to stand firm, and after all efforts to persuade him had failed, the exasperated bishop uttered his verdict: 'By the consent and counsel of my colleagues here present, I do pronounce thee, Thomas Bilney . . . to be convicted of heresy.' The public — even the king — wondered whether the new faith of the Cambridge scholar would stand the test of being threatened with death.

Three nights passed before Bilney was due for sentence, during which his friends crowded into his cell and pleaded with him to preserve his life. Weakened and sickened by the whole ordeal and demoralised by his friends Bilney suddenly broke down, signed the document of recantation and confessed his 'errors'. The result was public humiliation, in which he was made to lay a faggot on a bonfire of New Testaments and other Reformation books, plus twelve months imprisonment, and untold anguish of soul.

A distraught man emerged from prison the following year, for poor Bilney had lost his peace and communion with God. Nothing could comfort him. Like the apostle Peter, he had denied his Lord. By 1531, however, he gradually recovered his faith and came to the conclusion that there was only one course open to him to make amends for his failure. One evening, after saying goodbye to his friends in Cambridge, he set off into Norfolk to preach the faith in the open fields. He spoke to great crowds explaining God's way of forgiveness, attacking the superstitions of Rome, and openly repenting of his momentary denial of the biblical way of salvation. Wherever he went he also read publicly from Tyndale's New Testament, knowing full well what the outcome would be.

By July, Bilney had worked his way down to London, preaching everywhere. Then he went to Norwich where he continued to preach and distribute copies of the New Testament. This intensive programme of activity led to his being reported to Sir Thomas More, now Lord Chancellor in place of Wolsey, who ordered his arrest and imprisonment in the Tower of London. Thomas Bilney was taken back to Norwich for trial, and condemned to burn at the stake for heresy. Sir Thomas More — a fanatical Catholic who wholly approved the burning of 'heretics' — readily supplied the warrant. The day before his execution Bilney prepared himself by repeating the promise of God in *Isaiah 43.2 — When thou walkest through the fire, thou shalt not be burned; neither shall the flame kindle upon thee*. This, he said, meant that as the fire consumed the stubble of his body, the fire of the Holy Spirit could purify and take his soul, and he would enter into unspeakable joy.

On 19th August 1531, Bilney was escorted to the place where he was to be burned, called the Lollards' Pit, just outside the Norwich city wall. After confessing his faith to a deeply moved crowd, the slender figure of the Cambridge convert ascended the pile of wood and reeds reciting *Psalm 143*, repeating particularly the verse — *I stretch forth my hands unto thee: my soul thirsteth after thee, as a thirsty land.*

Foxe, the martyrologist, records: 'The sheriff's men then put the reeds and faggots about his body, and set fire to the reeds, which made a great blaze, and blackened his face; but the flames were blown away from him several times, the wind being very high, till at length, the wood taking fire, the flame was stronger, and so he yielded up the ghost.' The first Catholic priest to be converted to Christ in the English Reformation had joined the ranks of the Reformation martyrs, and gone to meet his Lord.

Less than four years later, in 1535, Tyndale was living in the house of a sympathetic merchant of Antwerp, having avoided his persecutors for years, when he was at last located by an agent from Britain, posing as a friend. Having won Tyndale's confidence, his hunter lured him to a dark alley where an ambush had been prepared. The Reformer was seized and taken bound to the Castle of Vilvorde near Brussels, where he was thrown into a stinking, rat-infested dungeon. After eighteen months Tyndale was put on trial for maintaining that faith in the Gospel is all that is required to obtain salvation, and for dismissing Catholic dogma. He was condemned as a heretic, unfrocked, excommunicated from the Church, and then in October 1536, led out for public execution. In the prison yard of the Castle of Vilvorde, after defying the final command to renounce his opinions, his gaunt, tired form was bound to a stake. Bystanders marvelled at his patience, and all heard the sympathetic tone of his last audible prayer, 'Lord, open the King of England's eyes.' First he was strangled with an iron chain, then his body was burned. William Tyndale, aged about 42, joined the martyr throng

Latimer preaching

having made the greatest contribution of any man to the translation of the Bible into English.

Hugh Latimer also suffered interrogation and temporary imprisonment — but the authorities had to be more careful with him for he had been appointed a royal chaplain in 1530, and preached frequently before the king, who held him in high regard. Latimer's persecutors were filled with dismay when, in 1535, Henry invited him to preach yet more sermons at Greenwich Palace, and appointed him Bishop of Worcester. With the protection of royal favour, Latimer preached ceaselessly round the country for four years, until Henry VIII compelled the clergy to submit to Roman Catholic doctrines as compulsory in the Church. Latimer opposed these measures, relinquished his bishopric, and was silenced for eight years, finally suffering arrest and confinement in the Tower until the young King Edward VI came to the throne in 1547.

Edward's accession marked a turning point for those who taught the biblical way of salvation. Latimer was released and for six years preached to the king and in every part of England as the principal evangelist among the Reformers. 'It was the sermons of Latimer,' said one noble historian, 'which more than any other factor established the principles of the Reformation in the minds and hearts of the people.' At the same time Cranmer, Ridley and others revised the teaching and worship of the Church.

The bishops and priests loyal to Rome saw their power destroyed, but they soon had an opportunity to re-establish Catholicism and to persecute and destroy biblical Christianity when the early death of Edward in 1553 brought Mary to the throne. Mary Tudor married Philip II of Spain and determined to restore the Roman Church in England. In doing so she had Hugh Latimer, Thomas Cranmer, Nicholas Ridley and almost 300 other leaders of the Reformation burned at the stake as heretics.

A warrant duly went out for Latimer's arrest, and he was brought to the Tower with Cranmer and Ridley and committed for trial. He was eventually led out for burning two years later in 1555, now eighty years of age. Together with Ridley he was chained to a stake in front of Balliol College, Oxford, with a bag of gunpowder round his neck and faggots piled about him. As the fire was lit, Latimer uttered his famous words, 'Be of good cheer, Master Ridley, and play the man; we shall this day, by God's grace, light such a candle in England, that shall never be put out.'

He was right. The retaliation of the Church of Rome did not survive for long. Believers in the Bible could be martyred, books could be burned, the clergy could be made to conform — *but the word of God is not bound (2 Timothy 2.9)*. The power at work in the land was the Bible, which continued to transform the spiritual attitude of hundreds of thousands of people as it worked in their minds and hearts. The land was set free from the superstition and darkness of medieval Romanism, and given the message of direct access to God by the work of Christ in dying for sinners.

It was not Henry VIII, or the bishops, or any other human power which brought the Reformation to England, for most were set against it. It was the power of the Scriptures bringing the meaning of true faith in Christ to the people, and so real was their discovery to all who found Christ — men, women, teenagers and little children also — that they were prepared even to burn, rather than deny their Lord.

The Making of a King
Alfred the Great

DENSE, DARK GREEN Berkshire woods surrounded
the long timber halls of the Saxon royal residence at
Wantage, England. Christmas had just passed and the
winter snow had given way to unrelenting drizzling
rain when a royal mother — gentle, deeply religious
Osburgh — gave birth to her fifth son, and called him
Alfred. The courtiers, servants and minstrels who
thronged the main hall thought they were celebrating
the birth of a minor prince; one who would never be
more than a sub-chief over a small district. They
could not have foreseen that he would become the
only Saxon whose name would resound down the
centuries, and the only English king to be known as
'the Great'. They could never have anticipated the
sweeping reforms, mighty victories and great innova-
tions which his reign produced.

The little prince came into a sorry domain. So much
was in a serious state of decline in the year 849. There
was no shortage of food and materials for everyone to
keep a good home, but community life was steadily
breaking down with the increase of brutality, larceny
and rape. Any semblance of education, even for
village elders and churchmen, had completely crum-

bled, and as for religious belief — scarcely a single flame of sincerity flickered amidst the pomp and show of an image-ridden, ritual-loving Church.

Alfred was introduced to the glamour and glitter of the medieval church at the tender age of four when he was taken to Rome to be baptised by Pope Leo IV. From the ancient port of Sandwich, through Paris, Lyons and across the Alps, his young eyes were opened wide with wonder at the sight of Rome, a rebuilt city of majestic, gleaming stonework. At home most buildings were wooden except for some rough, squat churches with narrow slits for windows. In Rome the little boy was crowned a Prince of the Church, but it was not an event he valued or even bothered to refer to in manhood. Perhaps his second visit to Rome only a year later stamped indelible memories on his young mind. By the time he and his father arrived in the city the old pope was dead, and people were fighting in the streets over the election of a successor. The cardinal eventually elected was seized and brutally attacked by the pious supporters of his defeated rival! Rome, for all her ornate buildings, learning, and droves of monks, was as clamorous and lawless a city as the worst Saxon community.

The little prince's mother died when he was only five and his father when he was eight. He therefore grew up without father or mother in the royal palaces of Wantage, Winchester, Oxford and Cheddar, surrounded by the rough influences of elder-courtiers, whose traditional role was to give a growing prince muscle and hunting skill. Along with most of his elder brothers they were a hardened, lustful, heavy-drinking crowd, none of whom were bestowed with any degree of intellectual capacity.

On a typical morning Alfred would emerge from

his bedroom to take breakfast in the Long Hall. All the royal homes had this curious, boat-shaped main room, with high beams supported by huge oak side pillars, between which hung richly coloured tapestries or curtains. Everyone and everything seemed to come into this room. The paved stone floor was strewn with items of hunting equipment; trestle-tables were laden with quantities of boiled pork and hot bread; members of the family mingled with courtiers and minstrels; wolfhounds held station under the tables; and trained hunting hawks housed themselves in the beams.

During the day a young prince was educated in the things that mattered in Saxon culture — the sports of leaping, wrestling, running and hunting. After an afternoon's hunting, the royal household would prepare for the evening banquet, and late into the night the Long Hall, lit by flaming torches, was filled with the stench of Saxon ale, and great roars of song.

By the age of thirteen Alfred began to stand out in the royal household as being cast in an unusual mould. The narrow, entirely physical emphasis of court life could not satisfy him, and he became intellectually very hungry. He began learning to read, although in the absence of any competent teachers his progress was painfully slow. But there was yet another aspect about this young prince which was different. Within himself he began to feel a deep shame and horror over wrong thoughts and deeds. It was a paralysing sensation of uncleanness which depressed him beyond description, and which he could not throw off.

Along with this he developed a craving to know about the future of a person's soul, particularly the eternal future of his own soul. When out hunting he would often turn aside into a deserted church to pray; and what prayers they were! Prostrate on the ground the prince would plead for relief from the burden of his sins. And yet he found to his dismay he would go on committing the same sins, fondling self-centred ambitions and desires, and wanting esteem and applause. His visits to the disused church became more frequent, until every morning when the cock crowed he would be out of bed and making for his familiar sanctuary. There he asked God to do something for him. He prayed to be made ardent in heart and mind, and for help to believe in God. He even prayed for some sickness to come to him so that he could be constantly reminded of his need for God.

As Alfred prayed, things began to happen which were unmistakably signs of God working within him. First, he developed a desire to *know* God personally. Then he discovered in a new way the meaning of the four Gospels. He learned that his burden of sin which weighed so heavily upon him could be taken away by Christ, Who had suffered and died on the cross to bear his due punishment. He found, in his youth, the truth about the atoning death of Christ for sinners, as expressed in a Saxon hymn, where Christ is made to say:—

> *How unequal was the reckoning between us two,*
> *When I received your pain, that you in bliss,*
> *Might happily enjoy my native realm.*

'To Thee I call,' Alfred prayed, 'Who cleanses us from all our sins and justifies us, and hears our prayers...' In answer to his prayer, the burden of his guilt was lifted from him. He knew that he was completely forgiven, and as he prayed day by day it seemed as though the Lord was an ever-present

Alfred's galleys attack Viking dragon ships, AD 891

friend. With great care he copied into a small book a selection of psalms, the services of the church, and a few prayers, and this book he carried with him everywhere as a source of help. He went off regularly to the little church he had come to know so well to pray alone.

In all this Alfred had little or no help from the royal chaplains, for the English Church at that time was a strange mixture. It was essentially Roman Catholic, but being a backward, out-of-the-way branch of the Church it was in some respects less advanced in corruption than the continental churches. Image worship had come in, along with confession to the priest, the founding of monasteries and the use of Latin services. But doctrines and practices such as the mass, transubstantiation, Mary worship and purgatory had not yet arrived, and married clergy were still the general rule. In addition, although the Saxon Church honoured the pope with gifts of money, he had no practical power or influence over its affairs. It was a church rich in images and ornaments, but almost entirely dead as far as spiritual life and power were concerned. Not surprisingly, when the Danish invasion swept the land, the Church suffered almost instantaneous collapse.

Shortly before the Danish invasion, Alfred, now a tall, blonde-haired young man, fell in love with a Mercian princess called Ealhswith, marrying her at Gainsborough amidst wild scenes of public delight. He was twenty-one when news came that the Danes had taken Thetford, defeated King Edmund and subdued East Anglia. Thousands of men were now advancing on Wessex, burning homesteads, looting churches, and slaughtering men, women and children without pity as they went. Flames roared into the sky from villages left in their wake.

Then they entered Saxon country, establishing a formidable base at Reading. Alfred was now crown prince and second in command of Saxon forces. At the famous Battle of Ashdown he scored a remarkable victory over the seemingly invincible Danes, securing for himself the complete respect of all his future subjects. In the battle, the Danes — who believed in an after-life where timid men were annihilated and the brave feasted for ever — took possession of a hilltop and waited for the conflict.

Alfred, whose army consisted of thousands of men whose homes had been smashed and whose families were scattered, immediately adopted tactics quite novel to his soldiers. Demanding strict discipline he formed his men into a dense body and stormed the hill. At the summit there was vicious hand-to-hand fighting. Equipped with small wooden shields, swords and axes, men hacked at each other to kill or be killed. So ferocious was the Saxon onslaught that the Danish defence broke and they retreated in disorder to their base camp at Reading. Prince Alfred was the hero of the day. The victory did not last, however, for as Danish reinforcements poured into the country from across the North Sea, the invaders soon gained the ascendancy. It was at the very height of this unprecedented national emergency that Alfred, aged 22, succeeded to the throne of England.

There was no frontier any more, for the country was overrun. Danes just had to be fought wherever they appeared, Alfred fighting nine major, exhausting battles in his first year as king. It was at this stage that he ordered the building of the first English naval vessels to fight Danes before they landed. It was probably also at this stage that the young king, being over-occupied by the war, and lifted up by the praise and flattery of his lieutenants, drifted from his spiritual moorings and abandoned faith in the Lord and prayer. Later, he wrote about a period of suffering and sin in his life when he went back to the ways of the world to achieve his desires, only to lose his peace and communion with God.

After seven long years of continual fighting, Alfred's exhausted men could hold out no longer. Battle-worn and outnumbered they were crushed into submission and the king had to take refuge in a wild, uncultivated swamp in Selwood Forest, Somerset. There, with a few troops, his little children and Ealhswith his devoted wife, Alfred recovered his spiritual strength. Perhaps it was at this moment of despair he wrote this poem:–

> *When in such strife my mind will forget*
> *Its light and its life, in worldly regret;*
> *And through the night of this world doth grope,*
> *Lost to the light of heavenly hope.*
>
> *Thus it has now befallen my mind,*
> *I know no more how God's goodness to find,*
> *But I groan in my grief, troubled and tossed,*
> *Needing relief, for the world I have lost!*

It must, surely, have been here that he prayed the prayer he afterwards wrote down:

'I implore Thee, Lord, to receive me, Thy fugitive, since once I was formerly Thine, and then deserted from Thee to the devil and fulfilled his will, enduring much misery in his service. But if to Thee it seems (as it does to me) that I have long enough endured the pains I have suffered, please receive me, Thine own servant. Never again let me go, now that I have sought Thee.' When the king's period of backsliding ended,

Alfred poses as a minstrel

he re-entered his experience of joy and peace, walking with the Lord.

The two best-known stories about Alfred come from the months he spent hiding in Selwood Forest — the burning of the cakes and the excursion into the Danish camp disguised as a minstrel. While they could well be true stories, they are widely considered to be colourful additions to the chronicles of Alfred's life.

The Saxon people generally were in a desperate condition. Most of them had become serfs to the Danes, and Alfred was presumed dead. So, when Easter came and the king unfurled his standard again with a call to arms, the people reacted with alacrity. A sudden, surprise attack was the sum total of Alfred's strategy, and the secret was well kept. By the time the Danes realised what was happening there was only time for fear. Alfred's men made a lightning dash to Chippenham, meeting their enemy at Edington. The Danish troops were completely routed and fled back to Chippenham where they surrendered after a four-teen-day siege. Sea-king Guthrum, their leader, even decided to embrace the Christian faith, no doubt in a rather superstitious, unenlightened way, as he experi-enced no apparent change of character.

It was a victory which gave King Alfred six years of peace so that he was able to turn his mind to the rebuilding of the social fabric of his country. But when he reviewed the state of England he hardly knew where to begin! So much needed to be done. His first major reform was the law of the land. Assault and immorality were defined as crimes for the first time; imprisonment was introduced; punishments simplified, and the statute book became logical and coherent as never before. Because Alfred's laws started with the Ten Commandments, Sabbath break-ing also became illegal for the first time in English law.

The king's palace itself underwent radical transfor-mation. Gone was the traditional bawdy, drunken Saxon court. The royal residence became a place where the head of state daily read the Bible with his wife and children. From here justice was regulated, poor relief liberally divided, and great reforms con-ceived and cradled. Also, from here words of life and light from the Latin Scriptures were translated into Anglo-Saxon for the people.

Alfred headed the church personally, introducing many reforms. Not only did he aim to get the words of Scripture to everyone, but he ordered the services to be read in the language of the people, commenced training schemes for the clergy, and rebuilt numerous tumbledown churches. The pope would hardly have approved the character of Alfred's rule in the Church, but the papacy of those days did not particularly care what happened in such far-flung regions as England so long as the monetary contributions continued to arrive. In the event, King Alfred appears to have stopped sending these in the last ten years of his reign.

After another terrible invasion by Danes in 885 had been successfully resisted, Alfred set to work designing and rebuilding a number of cities, including London. The next item on his agenda was an education programme, but this meant finding teachers. He secured the personal assistance of an able Welsh bishop named Asser, who later wrote the king's biography, and then sent overseas for teachers. Oxford University was revitalised, and schools were founded.

Soon he could write, 'So clear was knowledge fallen out of England that there were few on this side of the Humber who understood their service in English... and I cannot think of a single instance south of the Thames when I began to reign. Thanks be to God we now have some teachers...' Under his new rules all free-born youths, village elders and judges learned to read the English Scriptures. The school Alfred founded at Winchester was attended by his own children and he frequently taught there himself.

Alfred's personal contribution to the education programme was immense and largely spiritual. He accomplished the translation into Anglo-Saxon of six major Latin books, all being very free paraphrases with much original work. These included Christian authors such as Augustine, Bede's famous history, and a geographical work. He is credited with having translated a number of portions of Scripture, and to have almost completed his translation of the *Psalms* when he died.

Many of Alfred's widely-circulated poems are fervently evangelistic, such as the following verse:

Let him who is narrow and prisoned away
  By love of this earth so empty and vain,
Seek out for himself full freedom today
  That soul-feeding joys he may quickly attain.

Alfred had to endure the trials of two further invasions by the Danes before he drove them from English shores for the last time. With the Danes gone the great king had four quiet years, during which a painful illness that had harassed him from his early twenties grew considerably worse. He was only fifty-two when, conscious that he was approaching the end of his earthly course he called for his eldest son Edward and left his memorable commission:

'My son, I feel that my hour is near, my face is pale, and my days are nearly run. We must soon part. I shall go to another world and you shall be left alone with all my wealth. I ask you, for you are my dear child, strive to be a father and a lord to your people. Be the children's father and the widow's friend. Comfort the poor and shelter the weak and with all your might put right what is wrong. And, my son, govern yourself by the rules, then the Lord will love you and above all other things God will be your reward. Call upon Him to advise you in all your need and He shall help you all the more to accomplish all you intend.'

England was not to have another king approaching

Alfred's status or convictions for several centuries. Neither was there to be a church leader of his calibre for more than three centuries.

Hero of Malta
Lieut-General Sir William Dobbie

'THAT EXTRAORDINARY MAN General Dobbie,' was
how Churchill described him in Parliament. And in a
broadcast to the nation, he spoke of him as, 'General
Dobbie, for nearly two years the heroic defender of
Malta.' The historic siege and defence of Malta against
vastly superior forces during the Second World War
brought General Sir William Dobbie to well-deserved
fame.

He was born in Madras in 1879, the son of a high
official in the Indian Civil Service, and sent as a boy to
Charterhouse School, in England, for his education.
His parents were sincere Christian believers who had
brought him up to know the Bible. 'But the fact
remained,' General Dobbie recalled years later, 'that
in spite of their teaching, and in spite of the fact that I
knew God's plan of salvation in my head, it was not
until I was fourteen years old that I entered into the
spiritual experience which revolutionised my life. At
fourteen I came into a vital and saving contact with
the Son of God.'

This took place soon after the conversion of a
school friend, who wanted Dobbie to enter into the
same experience, and who took pains to explain to

him his new-found belief. Dobbie wrote, 'At that time God caused me to feel the weight of the burden of my sins. It was a heavy burden, a crushing burden, and one which made me feel miserable. I do not suppose that in the eyes of the world I was a particularly conspicuous sinner. I was, I imagine, much the same as most boys of my age, but I did realise that things were not right between God and me and that I was quite unfit to stand in His sight. I am more grateful than I can say that He put this burden on me. If He had not done so, I might never have sought for the relief which I found, and have found since increasingly, in Christ.

'Through the operation of the Holy Spirit, my need of a Saviour was brought home to me. On the first Sunday of November 1893, when I was spending a half-term holiday at Blackheath, I realised for the first time — although I had often heard it before — that Jesus Christ, the Son of God, had come to earth for the express purpose of laying down His life as the atonement for my sin, in order to deliver me from its penalty and power so that I might go free.

'I then and there accepted Jesus Christ as my Saviour, on the grounds that by His death, He had settled my debt once and for all. That was the turning point in my life. Having taken the great step, my first reaction was one of intense relief. The heavy burden was lifted for good. The past, black though it was in God's sight, was blotted out. Later, there came a feeling of gratitude to the One Who had brought this about, and amazement at the price He was willing to pay in order to make this possible. So also grew my desire to show my gratitude by obeying, following, pleasing, and acknowledging Him. In other words, He became not only my Saviour but also my Lord.'

At the age of eighteen Dobbie took the entrance examination of the Royal Military Academy at Woolwich and was offered a place. Then, having completed the two-year course, he was commissioned as a sub-lieutenant in the Royal Engineers. Being a thoughtful, unusually competent young man, he was soon selected for special training as a staff officer, and on the outbreak of the First World War was posted to France.

Dobbie spoke frequently of the many occasions on which he had received God's unmistakable help in particular difficulties. He was a praying man, and once described his experience of prayer in these words: 'It was like meeting an old friend in new circumstances, a friend who I had tested and proved times without number and who had never let me down.' During the 1914-18 war, Dobbie was promoted twice, first to the rank of major, then to that of lieutenant-colonel — created CMG, awarded the DSO and mentioned five times in despatches. After the war he served with the Rhine Army and spent several years at Aldershot as a staff officer. Then came promotion to full colonel and an intensely interesting and responsible post at the War Office.

Speaking about this time of his life, he said, 'I experienced the help of God in all sorts of circumstances. I saw His overruling control in my life and His guidance in my affairs. I have been amazed at His faithfulness to me in spite of much unfaithfulness on my part toward Him.'

Dobbie saw the events of 1928 as an example of the Lord overruling in the affairs of his life. He valued and enjoyed his post as a colonel at the War Office, particularly as a good War Office job usually served as a good pathway for one's future career. Then,

without warning, he was posted away from everything which seemed to matter and given a relatively
unimportant task at a very ordinary barracks at Chester. He was naturally disappointed and perplexed,
wondering why his prospects should change so
quickly. But there were further unseen changes ahead.
From Chester, he was soon promoted to command
the Cairo Brigade in Egypt, a promotion which
would not have been possible had he still been
stationed at the War Office.

From among all the commanders he was selected to
keep the peace in Palestine in the troubles of 1929. In
the summer of that year serious disturbances broke
out between Arabs and Jews. Troops and warships
were rushed in from Egypt, and Dobbie was sent to
command the combined operations of all three
services. He established his headquarters in Jerusalem
and acted with great speed, despatching troops to
emergency areas as soon as they arrived. However,
before the bulk of troops arrived he received a message that 5,000 armed Bedouin were travelling up to
attack the town of Gaza. At Gaza there was a large
population together with a mission hospital staffed by
British doctors and nurses with their families. If the
Bedouin entered Gaza the people would certainly be
murdered and the place reduced to a shambles. All
that Dobbie had available to send was a railway
engine coupled to a single truck carrying some mach-
ine guns. This could patrol the railway line which the
Bedouin would have to cross to get to Gaza, but what
an ineffective patrol it was likely to be! It could never
hope to locate and stop 5,000 tribesmen.

As time went by Dobbie received reports that the
Bedouin were getting nearer to Gaza. Then he turned
to his Saviour in prayer. 'I knelt and told Him that I

General and Mrs Dobbie landing at Malta

was at the end of my resources, and implored His help.' That evening, for no apparent reason, the Bedouin stopped their advance, changed direction and spent the night in open country. The following morning, *HMS Courageous* landed a battalion of troops in Jaffa, and Colonel Dobbie sent them straight to Gaza. The Bedouin delayed for just long enough for this battalion to take up position, and in the light of this strong defence force, a political officer persuaded the Bedouin to withdraw.

'Many a time,' wrote Dobbie, 'have I sought God's help and guidance in my official life, sometimes in small matters and sometimes in big ones, both in peace and war, and I can confidently assert that the promise of *James 1.5* is no idle or fanciful one. *If any of you lack wisdom, let him ask of God.* It is a wonderful reality ... providing one fulfils the conditions laid down.'

Dobbie successfully located the trouble-makers in Palestine and rounded them up before the violence escalated into national disorder. His outstanding success in organising the whole operation was rewarded by another honour — the CB, and when he was brought home from Cairo three years later he was promoted to major-general. General Dobbie served for three years as Commandant of the School of Military Engineering before going to Malaya as General Officer Commanding with the rank of lieutenant-general. There he stayed until 1939, when he was retired from active service, having passed his sixtieth birthday. When the Second World War broke out, William Dobbie was a retired general anxious to be able to serve in some way.

One day in April 1940, he had just finished lunch when he received word that General Sir Edmund Ironside wanted to see him. It was to ask this question: 'Will you go to Malta?' 'Certainly,' said General Dobbie, 'in what capacity?' 'As Governor,' came the reply. This was beyond all Dobbie's expectations. Nevertheless, just ten days after that interview, General Dobbie and his wife landed in Malta. Neither they nor the people at home in Britain realised what lay only a few weeks ahead.

At that time the British Empire stood alone against Germany — France having fallen — and the island fortress of Malta was a lonely British base only sixty miles from Sicily, and 1,000 miles from the nearest friendly base — Gibraltar. So, when Italy entered the war in the summer of 1940, on the side of Germany, Malta was plunged into the front line. She became an essential British base, to be held at all costs.

The Italians had boasted that they would capture Malta in a few days, and they began by heavy bombing of the island. The garrison defences were hopelessly inadequate. All Dobbie had at his disposal were five weak battalions, sixteen obsolete anti-aircraft guns, and the guns of *HMS Terror* in the harbour. London had nothing to send except a telegram from General Ironside. It read: 'Deuteronomy chapter 3 verse 22.' In the *Authorised Version* of the Bible the verse reads: *Ye shall not fear them: for the Lord your God he shall fight for you.*

General Dobbie, as Governor and Commander-in-Chief, issued a Special Order of the Day urging everyone to seek God's help and protection. There were no aircraft to defend Malta until four old Gloster Gladiator fighters were found in crates in the naval dockyard. These, flown by seaplane pilots who had no previous experience of fighters, were the sole aerial defence for three months.

On the ground, Dobbie organised defence measures for his crowded island of 270,000 people. Normally a military commander would have evacuated the women and children, but on Malta this was impossible. Conscription, rationing, rehousing and medical relief had to be arranged. Old underground tunnels were renovated and new ones dug for air raid shelters. The dockyard forges turned out thousands of picks, and miners excavated deep into the soft limestone until thirteen miles of new tunnels were

Clearing the rubble of the Valetta Opera House

complete. Dobbie — whose organising skills had been recognised so early by the army — inspired a level of ingenuity, efficiency and urgency which proved to be the key factor in the island's defence.

During two years of siege by Italian and German aircraft Malta sustained 2,000 bombing raids, destroying 37,000 buildings. *The Times* said, 'It is evident that the Germans are prepared to face almost any losses in their effort to reduce Malta to impotence. In this David and Goliath struggle, many aircraft are kept in Sicily to batter the island.' Despite all this and despite the fact that Malta was among the most densely populated places in the world, for every 200 people only one life was lost.

General Dobbie found it particularly noteworthy that the Italians never invaded Malta. 'It is a remarkable thing that the attempt was not made,' he said, 'especially in the early days of the siege when we were so weak... why? We are justified in asking another question. Why did not the Germans invade Great Britain immediately after Dunkirk? It seems that our two enemies each made a colossal blunder. The only reason which I can find and which seems to cover the facts is that in each case, God's restraining hand kept them from attacking us at a time when we were very ill-prepared to meet such an attack.'

As Governor of Malta, General Dobbie was known by the title 'His Excellency', and was housed in San Anton Palace. Part of his function was to preside over the daily proceedings of the Maltese Parliament. For General and Mrs Dobbie, however, home life at the palace was unpretentious and simple. The great feature of the palace routine was Dobbie's nightly, drawing-room prayer meeting. Many influential visitors to the island were struck by the earnestness and

General Dobbie takes the salute

sincerity of these times of prayer, when the Governor publicly brought before his Saviour all those on the island in his care.

The island Information Officer, Major Francis Gerard, said that there was no favouritism under Dobbie. 'All might expect a square deal. There would be no fear of any "palace clique" running the show. In point of fact when certain vested interests attempted to influence him they found themselves looking into a pair of very bleak blue eyes and heard the Governor return them an uncompromising "No". In the two years I was privileged to know him I never knew him do an unjust and an unkind thing. His courage and example were infectious. He was a big man — in every way.'

Personal courage was one of General Dobbie's special attributes. Some found it very uncomfortable to be with him when the bombing raids were at their worst because he would invariably make for a roof-top to watch the fate of his island. Under his style of leadership the morale of both the troops and the civilian population was kept exceptionally high. He frequently broadcast to the people over the island 'public address' system, and made no secret of his personal faith and dependence on God.

The bombing of Malta rose to a crescendo in April 1942. In that month over 100 aircraft were shot down by the anti-aircraft guns of the island. The following month General Dobbie was brought home to England. Prime minister Winston Churchill in a broadcast to the nation, said, 'We welcome back to our shores General Dobbie, for nearly two years the heroic defender of Malta.' The month before General Dobbie returned to England King George VI had written to him making the award of the George Cross to the whole island of Malta. When he arrived in London, he was received in audience by the king and knighted. The official statement about Dobbie's return read: 'In the dual office of Governor and Commander-in-Chief, Sir William Dobbie has been subjected to an immense strain in leading the defence of Malta...his leadership of the island fortress has won not only the confidence but the admiration of the Government.'

When the war was over Sir William addressed church gatherings and other public meetings all over the world telling of the things God had done in his own experience. To the nation, he wrote these words. 'In spite of the way God has been speaking to us in judgement and in mercy, we as a nation have not turned to Him...He is still largely crowded out of our lives and is ignored and disregarded by us — all this in spite of what He has done for us. May God open the eyes of our nation to see and open their ears to hear, and may we humbly acknowledge our sin and turn to Him.'

Of his own experience walking with Christ down the years, he wrote: 'Often I have grieved and disappointed Him. And yet, through it all, I am amazed at His forbearance and kindness to me. These thoughts create...an intense feeling of gratitude to the One Who has stood by me in spite of all. I desire to emphasise, especially to the rising generation, that it is a practical and intensely real thing to let Christ come into one's life, and today, as ever before, it is no vain thing to trust in the living God.'